Type 2 Diabetes Cookbook for Beginners

Rediscover the Joy of Cooking: A World of Diabetes-Friendly Recipes, Meticulously Crafted with a Transformative 28-Day Meal Plan for Every Kitchen Skill Level

EMMA SAGE

TABLE OF CONTENTS

Introduction: Understanding Type 2 Diabetes

Welcome to a comprehensive exploration of type 2 diabetes, a journey designed to enlighten, inform, and empower individuals from all corners of the globe. With its far-reaching impact, this ailment necessitates an in-depth grasp of effective management, regardless of geographical or cultural context.

At the crux of type 2 diabetes is a metabolic dysfunction characterized by the body's inability to efficiently utilize or produce insulin, the hormone responsible for glucose metabolism. The result is an elevated blood sugar level, which, over time, can incur extensive systemic ramifications.

Effective management goes beyond merely controlling blood sugar. It delves into the intricate dance of macronutrients—carbohydrates, proteins, and fats—and their subsequent influence on glycemic responses. The end goal is more than just stable blood sugar levels; it's optimizing overall metabolic health.

Transitioning to a diabetic-friendly diet doesn't necessitate a drastic overnight transformation. Evidence suggests that a phased approach, built upon consistent, informed choices, yields more sustainable results. Deciphering food labels, for instance, is a critical skill. It's about navigating the maze of nutritional information, distinguishing between beneficial and detrimental fats, and being vigilant of concealed sugars.

Consistency is paramount. The human body, with its intricate systems, thrives on regularity. This includes not just what you consume but also when you consume it. Timely meals can substantially mitigate the risk of glycemic anomalies. Furthermore, intertwining dietary practices with physical activity enhances insulin sensitivity, offering a two-pronged advantage.

In subsequent chapters, we will meticulously dissect the nuances of diet, physical activity, and the overall lifestyle of type 2 diabetes. This isn't merely a culinary guide; it's a scientifically backed manual interwoven with real-life narratives, experiences, and strategies. Embark on this journey with me, harnessing knowledge to transform it into proactive action. Your metabolic health awaits your empowered choices.

Chapter 1: Beyond the Plate: Managing Type 2 Diabetes

The Importance of Proactive Diabetes Management

In health and wellness, type 2 diabetes is a condition that demands undivided attention. Every dietary choice influences the body's balance between insulin and glucose. To manage this ailment effectively, being proactive is essential, shaping decisions, prioritizing health, and preventing complications.

Often, there's a misconception that managing diabetes solely involves avoiding certain foods. In reality, proactive management emphasizes the positive actions one can take. For instance, rather than simply avoiding a sugar-laden pastry for breakfast, it's about consciously selecting a nutritious omelet filled with vegetables. This choice avoids sugar and provides sustained energy from protein and fiber.

Managing diabetes proactively means preempting challenges. By understanding how different foods influence blood sugar, individuals can make informed decisions that prevent undesired fluctuations. Moreover, incorporating habits like regular blood sugar monitoring can reveal patterns, allowing for more targeted interventions. Adding regular exercise, even something as simple as a brisk walk, can enhance the body's ability to regulate insulin and glucose, further aiding in managing the condition.

Beyond the physical advantages, proactive management offers psychological benefits. By taking control, individuals reduce the uncertainty and anxiety associated with diabetes. Instead of reacting to health challenges as they arise, they can operate from a position of empowerment, leading to enhanced mental well-being.

The long-term implications of proactive management must be considered. Regularly having high blood sugar may not appear harmful at first, but over time, it can cause serious issues that affect many organs and systems. By being proactive, individuals enhance their daily quality of life and pave the way for a healthier future.

In conclusion, managing type 2 diabetes requires foresight and informed decisions. It's not merely about restrictions but about taking positive, purposeful actions. Every step taken with intention and knowledge can profoundly impact overall well-being, ensuring a life of health and vitality.

Type 2 Diabetes Explained: Definition and Physiological Impact

Type 2 diabetes is more than just a term or a condition. It's a significant life alteration, a silent reminder that our bodies are vast and intricate systems requiring a balance not always easily achieved. So, what exactly is type 2 diabetes, and why is its understanding crucial for those diagnosed and their families?

The hallmark of type 2 diabetes is the body's incapacity to use insulin, a hormone that is in charge of delivering glucose—our primary energy source—from the bloodstream into the cells. In essence, our body becomes resistant to the effects of insulin, requiring more of it to get the same glucose-transporting job done. But our insulin-producing cells can't keep up with this heightened demand over time. The result? Elevated blood sugar levels.

You might think, "What's a little extra sugar in the blood?" But the truth is that consistently elevated blood sugar can have ripple effects across various bodily systems. Here's the crux of the matter:

Vascular System: High blood sugar can damage blood vessels, making them more susceptible to atherosclerosis, a hardening and narrowing of the arteries. This impediment can lead to heart disease and an increased risk of stroke.

Nervous System: The excess sugar can also harm the exemplary network of nerves in our body, especially in the extremities, like feet. Known as neuropathy, this condition can result in numbness, tingling, or even pain.

Kidneys: Acting as our body's filtration system, kidneys can get overwhelmed by the constant barrage of sugar, leading to kidney disease or even kidney failure in severe cases.

Eyes: High blood sugar affects the tiny blood vessels in the eyes, potentially leading to conditions like diabetic retinopathy, which can cause vision impairment or even blindness.

Digestive System: Gastroparesis is a condition where the stomach delays emptying its contents, a complication arising from nerve damage due to prolonged high blood sugar.

The human body operates in a delicate balance, and the physiological impacts of type 2 diabetes underscore this. It's not just about numbers on a glucose meter; it's about the fabric of our being, our daily experiences, and our interactions with the world.

While it's paramount to understand the physical ramifications, we mustn't underestimate the emotional and psychological toll. The diagnosis can be a shock, leading to denial, anger, and sadness. Over time, the constant need for vigilance – monitoring blood sugar, watching diet, ensuring regular exercise – can be mentally exhausting. Moreover, the fear of potential complications, from vision loss to kidney problems, can be a significant source of anxiety.

However, knowledge is empowerment. By understanding type 2 diabetes, its origins, and its impacts, individuals can approach their condition with clarity, determination, and hope. It's not just about managing symptoms; it's about reclaiming life, embracing every moment with informed decisions, and confidently navigating the journey.

Knowledge fosters compassion. For family and friends, understanding the condition means supporting their loved ones physically and emotionally. It means recognizing the challenges, being there during the lows, and celebrating the highs. After all, every step taken toward understanding is a step toward a brighter, healthier tomorrow.

Diet's Role in Diabetes: Food's Effect on Blood Sugar and the Concept of Balanced Meals

The intricate relationship between diet and diabetes, precisely Type 2 diabetes, has been the subject of extensive research over the past decades. Type 2 diabetes, at its core, is a chronic metabolic illness characterized by a relative lack of insulin and insulin resistance, a state in which the body's cells cannot react appropriately to the insulin hormone.

From a physiological standpoint, when we consume food, mainly those rich in carbohydrates, they are metabolized into glucose – a primary energy source for the body's cells. In response, the hormone insulin is released by the pancreatic beta cells. Insulin encourages the uptake of glucose into cells and provides them with the energy they need to function. But in Type 2 diabetes, this glucose regulation is impaired. The cellular insulin response is diminished, leading to hyperglycemia or elevated blood glucose levels. Sustained hyperglycemia is detrimental, leading to potential microvascular (like neuropathy, nephropathy, retinopathy) and macrovascular complications (like heart disease).

This brings into focus the paramount importance of diet in diabetes management. It's not just about calorie counting; it's about understanding foods' glycemic load and glycemic index and how they can impact blood sugar. A system called the glycemic index (GI) is used to rate foods high in carbohydrates according to how much more they raise blood glucose levels than a typical meal. A portion of food's GI and carbohydrate content are taken into account by the glycemic load (GL), which provides a more complete picture of the food's possible effects on blood sugar levels.

However, it's essential to understand the role of other macronutrients beyond carbohydrates. Proteins, for instance, are pivotal for cellular repair and growth and can also modulate the postprandial glycemic response when consumed with carbohydrates. Dietary fats, especially polyunsaturated and monounsaturated fats, can enhance cell membrane fluidity, potentially improving cell response to insulin.

For people with Type 2 diabetes, dietary intervention takes many forms. It encompasses selecting nutrient-dense foods, understanding the complexities of macronutrient interactions, and ensuring a regular meal pattern to prevent erratic glucose fluctuations. Consuming high-fiber foods, like whole grains, legumes, and certain fruits, can mitigate rapid glucose spikes, offering more controlled glycemic responses. Moreover, integrating lean protein sources and beneficial fats ensures comprehensive nourishment, improving overall metabolic health.

Conclusively, the intricate dance between dietary intake and glucose homeostasis in Type 2 diabetes underscores the need for personalized nutritional strategies. Through informed dietary choices, rigorous monitoring, and an understanding of the physiological underpinnings, individuals can effectively navigate the challenges posed by this metabolic disorder, ensuring optimal health outcomes.

Simple Steps to Change: Gradual Dietary Modifications and Goal Setting

In managing Type 2 Diabetes, the initial phase is often the most challenging. Those accustomed to certain eating habits for years suddenly must change their diet. But diving into the cognitive processes that underscore change can make this transition smoother.

It's widely recognized in behavioral sciences that meaningful change only happens after some time. In the behavioral sciences, it is commonly acknowledged that significant change takes time to manifest. According to Carlo DiClemente and James Prochaska's Transtheoretical Model, developed in the 1970s, behavioral adaptation occurs gradually. From pre-contemplation to contemplation, preparation, action, maintenance, and finally termination, every individual undergoes a journey of understanding and acceptance. When it comes to Type 2 Diabetes, many patients meander through these stages, sometimes stuck in contemplation, uncertain of how to make tangible preparations or take definitive actions.

Receiving a diagnosis of Type 2 Diabetes doesn't compel a person to radically shift their diet immediately. Severe dietary changes can occasionally backfire, increasing the likelihood of reverting to old habits and causing feelings of deprivation.To effectively manage diabetes, one must be aware of the Glycemic Index, which grades foods based on how much blood they elevate. Dr. David Jenkins, the mind behind this concept, stresses its importance. But diving headfirst into distinguishing between high and low-GI foods can be daunting. A gentler strategy is to introduce one new low-GI food a week. A patient could start by learning about quinoa's benefits and slowly adding it to their diet, realizing over time that it's a healthier alternative to white rice.

Similarly, understanding and tweaking portion sizes can be transformative. By cutting down carbohydrate portions by about 20% and introducing more lean proteins, patients can notice significant improvements in their post-meal glucose levels. Simple modifications, like substituting a piece of spaghetti with grilled chicken or tofu, can yield considerable benefits.

While the physiological aspect of diabetes management is crucial, the psychological facet is equally, if not more, significant. Transforming abstract advice like "manage your blood glucose levels" into specific, actionable goals can make a difference. Setting clear, measurable, and timely goals, such as transitioning to whole-grain toast over two weeks to reduce post-breakfast glucose spikes, can lead to more sustainable habits. Furthermore, patients must know that indulging occasionally is okay, as long as they compensate with activities like a slightly longer walk the next day or a stricter meal plan.

Consistent consultations with endocrinologists and dietitians are pivotal. These experts guide adjusting medications and offer invaluable insights into diet optimization. Keeping a food journal and reflecting on dietary choices can help patients understand their glucose fluctuations better. By keeping a dynamic approach tailored to individual needs and lifestyles, patients can find their own unique path to managing their condition.

In essence, managing Type 2 Diabetes through dietary modifications is a journey of consistent, deliberate steps. Patients can achieve physical well-being and mental and emotional balance by understanding change, taking a phased approach to nutritional shifts, setting clear goals, and regularly consulting and adjusting based on feedback. This holistic path ensures a harmonious relationship between the body and mind.

Reading Food Labels: A Quick Guide to Understanding Crucial Components

Navigating the labyrinthine world of food labels is more than just a rite of passage for individuals diagnosed with Type 2 Diabetes; it's necessary. Recognizing the nuances in food labels is akin to deciphering a foreign language. However, with time, persistence, and understanding, this process becomes second nature, empowering patients to make informed decisions.

Decoding Nutritional Facts

When picking up packaged food products, the most important thing to look for is the "Nutrition Facts" panel. This section provides a breakdown of essential nutrients per serving. Let's delve deeper.

Carbohydrates: are the chief concern for people with diabetes. Carbs, when ingested, break down into sugars. Under this category, focus on 'Total Carbohydrates,' which includes fibers, sugars, and starches. Additionally, look at 'Sugars' (naturally occurring or added) and 'Dietary Fiber' (aim for products with higher fiber).

Calories: While this indicates the energy a food provides, it's pivotal to determine where these calories originate. For instance, 150 calories from a candy bar (primarily sugars) versus 150 calories from a handful of nuts (comprising proteins and healthy fats) can vastly impact glucose levels.

Fats: Though not directly related to blood sugar, fats can affect insulin sensitivity. Differentiate between types of fats. Trans fats and saturated fats are less desirable due to potential cardiovascular concerns, whereas fish, nuts, and olive oil are good sources of mono and polyunsaturated fats.

Although protein can affect blood sugar, especially when consumed in excess, it is necessary for tissue repair and muscle growth.

Sodium: While not a direct concern for blood sugar, those with diabetes often have an increased risk of hypertension. Maintaining a sodium-conscious diet helps in overall health management.

Serving Size and Servings Per Container
At the top of the label, these two metrics are crucial. Misinterpreting them can significantly impact blood glucose. If a packet says it contains three servings and you consume the entire content, you're ingesting three times the listed nutrients.

Ingredients List: The Art of Discernment
While the nutrition facts panel provides quantitative information, the ingredient list offers qualitative insights. An ingredient list is presented in descending order of weight.

Watch out for sugars disguised under myriad names: maltose, dextrose, fructose, corn syrup, and many others. The higher up they appear, the more sugar the product contains. Conversely, terms like 'whole grain' or'sprouted' appearing early in the list indicate a healthier carbohydrate source.

Allergens and Additives
Being mindful of allergens and additives is paramount for many, especially those on specific medications or with secondary health concerns. Manufacturers typically highlight common allergens, but it's always safe to scrutinize the ingredient list.

The Reality of Marketing Terms
"Natural," "Light," and "Low-"Fat"—these terms can be misleading. For instance, a "natural" product might still contain sugars. It's always prudent to cross-check the nutrition facts and ingredient list.

Embracing the role of a discerning consumer, armed with knowledge and vigilance, is an integral part of managing Type 2 Diabetes. Remember, every bite you take is a data point in the grand scheme of your health. While the initial steps might seem overwhelming, they pave the way to autonomy, confidence, and a sustainable, health-conscious lifestyle. The more you familiarize yourself with labels, the better you can customize your diet, keeping you not just in control of your diabetes but truly thriving with it.

Meal Planning Basics: Benefits, a Sample Meal Plan, and Shopping Tips

When managing Type 2 diabetes, what's on your plate plays a pivotal role. And here's where meal planning is essential to guide food choices, ensuring you receive a balance of nutrients while keeping blood sugar levels in check.

Efficiency in Daily Life: With a clear plan, you're not left wondering what to cook or eat next. This clarity can save time and mental energy, especially in our fast-paced lives.

Diversifying Your Diet: A well-thought-out plan ensures you're not repeatedly consuming the same foods. This variety is good for the palate and provides nutrients from different sources.

Alleviating Mental Load: We often underestimate the mental strain of making decisions, especially concerning our health. A planned meal system removes the daily burden, offering peace of mind.

A Tailored Diabetes-Friendly Meal Plan

Breakfast: A warm bowl of oatmeal topped with fresh blueberries and a sprinkle of flaxseeds partnered with an herbal tea.

Lunch: Lentil soup, rich in protein and fiber, and a slice of whole-grain bread.

Afternoon Snack: A handful of carrot sticks with a hummus dip.

Dinner: Stir-fried tofu with colorful bell peppers, zucchini, and snap peas in olive oil, sprinkled with sesame seeds. Finish with a small serving of fresh fruit salad.

Evening Snack: A cup of chamomile tea with a couple of almonds.

This layout is illustrative. Everyone's body and needs are unique, and engaging with a healthcare professional to refine and adjust your meal strategy is always recommended.

Constructing a Diabetes-Friendly Shopping List

When heading to the grocery store, being armed with a shopping list tailored to diabetic needs can be beneficial. Here's a sample:

Proteins: Tofu, lentils, chicken breast, salmon, and eggs.

Grains and Cereals: Whole grain bread, brown rice, quinoa, and steel-cut oats.

Vegetables: Spinach, bell peppers, zucchini, broccoli, and carrots.

Fruits: Blueberries, apples, kiwis, and strawberries.

Dairy or Alternatives: Greek yogurt, almond milk, and feta cheese.

Snacks & Others: Hummus, flaxseeds, almonds, olive oil, and herbal teas.

Pragmatic Tips for Shopping Smart

Limit Distractions: Focus on your list. Grocery stores are designed to entice buyers into unplanned purchases. Stick to your plan.

Be Season-Wise: Seasonal fruits and vegetables are fresher and often cheaper. They add variety to your meals and align with nature's cycles.

Stay Informed & Updated: New products continuously emerge in the market. Keep updated about diabetic-friendly products, but always approach them with a critical eye. If unsure, it's best to consult a diabetes expert or nutritionist.

In managing diabetes, it's not just about monitoring glucose levels but ensuring that every meal is a step towards better health. Through strategic meal planning and smart shopping, living with diabetes can be manageable and enjoyable.

Consistent Meal Timing: Its Importance and Strategies for Regularity

Understanding our body's circadian rhythm and how it interacts with food can be a game changer when managing Type 2 diabetes. This biological clock influences various physiological processes, including the secretion of insulin, an essential hormone in glucose metabolism. Regular meal timing harmonizes with this internal clock, leading to optimized blood sugar control and better overall health. But why is consistency in meal timing so critical, and how can we ensure regularity?

The Synchronization of Insulin and Glucose

Blood glucose levels increase in people with Type 2 diabetes after eating, particularly when they consume carbohydrates. To aid cells in absorbing this glucose, the pancreas secretes insulin in response. On the other hand, this insulin response may be inadequate or delayed in people with Type 2 diabetes. Eating meals at regular intervals helps us anticipate and control these blood glucose spikes. This consistency makes sure that there isn't an abrupt spike in glucose, which could overburden the already weakened insulin response.

Physiological Harmony and Enhanced Digestion

Consistency in meal timing also facilitates better digestion. The gastrointestinal system anticipates meals, preparing to digest and absorb nutrients. Eating meals erratically disrupts this preparation, potentially leading to indigestion or suboptimal nutrient absorption. Furthermore, consistent meal timing can aid satiety signals, helping to avoid overeating or unnecessary snacking, further complicating blood sugar management.

Strategies for Ensuring Regular Meal Timing

1. Understand Your Body's Signals: Initially, you might need to recalibrate your hunger signals. Observe when you naturally feel hungry, and try to schedule meals around these times. This personal introspection can lay the foundation for setting a meal schedule.

2. Plan: Plan meal timings as you would with meal content. If your lunch is regularly at noon, try to keep it that way. Set reminders or alarms to keep yourself on track, especially in the beginning.

3. Stay Prepared: Life can be unpredictable. Keeping a small, balanced snack on hand can prevent long gaps between meals if unforeseen circumstances delay your regular mealtime.

4. Evaluate and Adjust: If you find a particular time isn't working, make adjustments. Perhaps your dinner is too late, and you're not hungry for breakfast. Consider moving feed earlier, ensuring you're hungry when you wake.

5. Consult with a Diabetologist: Every individual's response to food and insulin can vary. Regular consultations with a diabetologist can help fine-tune your meal timings based on your blood sugar readings.

Timing of meals consistently has a significant impact on blood sugar regulation and general health. It makes sure that all of your body's internal processes—from digestion to insulin secretion—coordinate with your eating patterns. This combination has the potential to be the key to a healthier, more balanced life for people with Type 2 diabetes.

Physical Activity's Role: Importance and Beginner-Friendly Exercise Suggestions

Managing type 2 diabetes involves a holistic approach that combines dietary measures, medication, regular monitoring, and another equally important component - physical activity. Integrating exercise into one's routine can profoundly affect glucose control, and understanding the underlying science can genuinely transform how one approaches diabetes management.

When an individual engages in physical activity, the muscles are put to work. These muscles actively consume glucose as energy, leading to a natural and effective decrease in circulating blood sugar levels. Furthermore, exercise has a profound effect on improving insulin sensitivity. In simple terms, post-exercise, our body's cells are more receptive to insulin, enabling more efficient glucose uptake from the bloodstream. This heightened insulin sensitivity can persist for more than 24 hours post-exercise, offering a prolonged window of improved glucose control.

Moreover, physical activity plays a pivotal role in weight management. It's well-established that obesity, particularly central obesity, is a significant risk factor for insulin resistance. By shedding extra weight, the body can better respond to insulin, allowing for more efficient glucose regulation.

Now, for those living with type 2 diabetes and pondering where to start, it's crucial to emphasize that the exercise regimen should be practical and sustainable. Jumping straight into high-intensity workouts might not be feasible or safe. Instead, gradual integration of exercise into daily routines is the key.

Walking is an excellent starting point. A simple stroll in the park or around the block can make a difference. To make this more practical for glucose management, consider timing these walks post meals, particularly after consuming a carbohydrate-rich meal. This can assist in offsetting potential spikes in blood sugar.

Resistance exercises can benefit those keen on building muscle strength, pivotal for boosting metabolic rates and improving muscle glucose storage capacity. This doesn't necessarily mean heavy weight lifting. Resistance bands or body-weight exercises, like squats and push-ups, can be influential. For example, a routine consisting of three sets of ten squats, push-ups, and lunges every alternate day can be a practical starting point.

Lastly, activities that enhance flexibility and balance, like Tai Chi or basic yoga postures, can be particularly beneficial. Not only do they promote physical well-being, but they also offer mental relaxation, which is crucial for managing stress-induced blood sugar fluctuations.

While the journey with type 2 diabetes can seem challenging, incorporating physical activity offers a proactive tool to regain control. It's not just about the numbers on the glucose meter; it's about overall well-being, empowerment, and leading a balanced, healthy life.

Chapter 2: The Importance of Diet in Managing Blood Sugar

Diet: A Pillar of Blood Sugar Regulation

At the heart of every person living with type 2 diabetes is a continuous quest: maintaining stable blood glucose levels. The food you consume serves as the foundational pillar in this journey. While medications and other interventions play a role, your dietary habits can significantly steer the course of your condition.

The Subtleties of Carbohydrates: Quality Over Quantity

The relationship between carbohydrates and blood sugar isn't just about quantity but, more critically, quality. While carbohydrates convert into glucose, different carb sources have varying impacts on blood sugar levels.

Whole grains, for instance, have complex structures. Their intricate makeup requires more time for the digestive system to process, ensuring a slower and more manageable release of glucose. Imagine a water dam; you want a controlled, consistent flow instead of a sudden rush.

In contrast, processed foods, often stripped of their natural nutrients and fibers, quickly break down, causing abrupt spikes in glucose levels. Such peaks can strain the pancreas and increase insulin resistance over time.

A Balanced Plate: Beyond Carbohydrates

While carbohydrates often become the focal point in diabetes discussions, a holistic dietary approach encompasses more. Proteins and fats, for instance, can act as buffers, moderating how quickly carbohydrates are digested and glucose is released.

Including a lean protein source, such as grilled chicken or tofu, alongside healthy fats like those found in olive oil or almonds can create a satiating meal. This not only aids in blood sugar management but also curbs unnecessary snacking, which can disrupt glucose stability.

Variety: The Spice of Dietary Management

Getting caught in a dietary rut is easy, especially when trying to manage a medical condition. However, the world of diabetic-friendly foods is vast and flavorful. Embracing variety ensures a broader spectrum of nutrients, making blood sugar management more efficient and less monotonous. For instance, occasionally swapping quinoa for brown rice can offer a different nutrient profile, preventing potential deficiencies.

Staying Informed, Staying Empowered

Knowledge is the cornerstone of adequate blood sugar management. The more you understand the nuances of food and its impact on your body, the better you'll be able to make beneficial choices. Whether selecting ingredients for a home-cooked meal or navigating a restaurant menu, informed decisions can empower you, ensuring that type 2 diabetes remains a manageable aspect of your life.

Chapter 3: Tailoring Your Diet: The Basics

Addressing dietary habits with the lens of type 2 diabetes requires a nuanced understanding of how foods influence blood sugar. Different foods, even within the same category, can affect glucose levels differently. This knowledge allows for making informed choices that can significantly improve glycemic control. Let's explore some scenarios:

Breakfast Choices

A morning meal often sets the tone for the day. While many cereals, even those labeled as "healthy," can cause a surge in blood sugar due to their high carbohydrate content, opting for protein-rich alternatives can make a difference. For instance, instead of a cereal bowl, considering a combination of Greek yogurt, mixed nuts, and a controlled portion of fruit can stabilize blood sugar. The protein and healthy fats slow down the absorption of sugars, leading to a more balanced glycemic response.

Lunch Variations

The convenience of grabbing a sandwich often makes it a popular choice for lunch. However, the type of bread and fillings can influence its impact on blood sugar. Choosing whole-grain bread over white bread provides complex carbohydrates that are digested slower, offering a steady release of glucose. Additionally, incorporating more vegetables into the sandwich increases fiber, further moderating blood sugar spikes.

Smart Snacking

Snacking can be a challenge, especially when most ready-to-eat options are carb-heavy. Instead of reaching for a granola bar or pack of crackers, considering alternatives like hummus with vegetable sticks or a handful of mixed nuts can be beneficial. These protein and fiber-rich options keep you satiated and prevent sharp rises in glucose.

Dinner Dynamics

Balancing carbohydrates with proteins and fats is essential for those who enjoy a hearty dinner. A pasta meal, while delicious, can influence glucose levels significantly. However, incorporating whole-grain pasta, reducing the portion size, and adding a protein source, legumes for vegetarians, or lean meat for others can optimize the meal. Furthermore, introducing more vegetables or considering alternatives like spiralized vegetables can reduce the carbohydrate load.

Post-Exercise Nutrition

After a good workout, rewarding oneself with a fruit-rich smoothie or energy bar is tempting. However, being selective is crucial. Opting for low-glycemic fruits like berries, adding leafy greens, or including seeds like chia or flax can offer nutritional benefits without causing glucose spikes. If you prefer an energy bar, look for those with a good balance of protein, fats, and minimal added sugars.

The Importance of Stable Blood Sugar Before Bed

Balanced Evening Meals: Your dinner should balance protein, healthy fats, and complex carbohydrates. This helps gradually release glucose at night, preventing sudden spikes or drops.

Limit Simple Sugars: Prevent eating desserts or snacks that are high in simple sugars before bed. Rapid blood sugar spikes may result from them, and if this happens at night, blood sugar may drop and hypoglycemia may develop.

Consider a Bedtime Snack

Protein and Fat: If you often experience nighttime hypoglycemia, a small snack rich in protein and fat might be beneficial before sleeping. This could be a spoonful of almond butter or a small piece of cheese.

Mind Your Medications

Timing Matters: Some diabetes medications can cause hypoglycemia. Discuss with your healthcare provider the best times to take them, especially if you're on multiple daily doses.

Ensure a Good Night's Sleep

Regular Sleep Schedule: Consistency is critical. Going to bed and waking up at the same time daily can stabilize circadian rhythms and improve insulin sensitivity.

Reduce Screen Time: The hormone that induces sleep, melatonin, can be disrupted by the blue light that comes from computers, phones, and tablets. Aim to unplug at least one hour before going to bed.

Key Is Comfort: Make sure you have a comfortable place to sleep. Darkness, the ideal room temperature, and a comfortable mattress are all part of this. Think about using an eye mask or blackout curtains if necessary.

Control Your Stress: High stress can interfere with sleep and have an impact on blood sugar. Before going to bed, think about practicing relaxation methods like deep breathing, meditation, or reading a soothing book.

Be Prepared

Nightstand Essentials: Keep a glucose meter, a source of quick-acting sugar (like glucose tablets or a juice box), and water by your bedside. This ensures you're prepared if you wake up feeling the symptoms of low blood sugar.

Stay Hydrated, but Be Cautious: High blood sugar can cause frequent urination, potentially disrupting sleep. While it's essential to stay hydrated, limit excessive fluid intake before bed to avoid multiple nighttime trips to the bathroom.

Monitor Blood Sugar Regularly: If your blood sugar is high or low when you wake up, it may be related to your sleeping patterns or the medications you take. You can spot patterns and make necessary adjustments by regularly monitoring them.

Remember, while these tips are general guidelines, individual needs can vary. It's always beneficial to consult with a healthcare professional or diabetes educator about personalized strategies for nighttime management.

Chapter 4: Safe Sweeteners and Carbohydrate Awareness

When discussing diabetes and diet, carbohydrates inevitably become a cornerstone of the conversation. Carbohydrates in many foods break down into glucose in our bloodstream. Managing and understanding their intake is pivotal for those with diabetes. While carbohydrate awareness is crucial, addressing the sweet tooth without exacerbating blood sugar levels becomes an equally important challenge. Here's a deep dive into sweeteners and their intersection with carbohydrate consciousness.

Carbohydrates Briefly Explained

Carbohydrates serve as our body's primary energy source. They're categorized into simple (sugars) and complex (starches and fiber) carbs. For someone with diabetes, recognizing the difference is essential. Simple carbohydrates in fruits, milk, and sugar-laden products can rapidly increase blood glucose. Conversely, complex carbohydrates in whole grains, legumes, and vegetables release glucose slowly, providing sustained energy and less immediate impact on blood sugar.

Navigating Through the Sweetening Spectrum

As sweeteners have become integral to our dietary landscape, knowing their potential effects on diabetes is vital.

Natural Sweeteners: Nature's Sweet Gifts

Stevia: A power-packed leaf extract, Stevia brings sweetness without the carbohydrate baggage. Its non-caloric nature means it doesn't impact blood glucose, but remember, a little goes a long way.

Monk Fruit: Sharing the spotlight with Stevia, Monk fruit offers sweetness without the glycemic response. However, it is crucial to ensure that it hasn't been blended with other high-glycemic sweeteners in commercial preparations.

Agave Nectar: Although a natural source, its high fructose content warrants caution. While it doesn't cause instant spikes in blood sugar, excessive intake might have long-term metabolic consequences.

Artificial Sweeteners: Man-made Sugar Alternatives

Aspartame: A frequent occupant in diet sodas, aspartame doesn't raise blood glucose. However, its continuous consumption and potential side effects remain debated topics among experts.

Sucralose: This heat-stable sweetener often graces baked goods. It's carb-free, but some might find its taste profile less appealing.

Saccharin: Its historical roots make it a known entity. Although it doesn't impact blood sugar, consuming it in moderation is advisable, keeping potential digestive issues in mind.

Carbohydrate Awareness in Sweetened Products

Products labeled 'sugar-free' can be misleading. The absence of sugar doesn't guarantee a low-carbohydrate profile. Ingredients like maltodextrin, dextrose, and maltose might lie in wait, ready to affect blood glucose. Always be a diligent reader of nutritional labels.

Chapter 5: Recipes for Breakfast

Recipe 1: Almond Flour Pancakes with Berry Compote

P.T. = 20 minutes

Ingr. = 1 cup almond flour, 2 big eggs, 1/4 cup unsweetened. almond milk, 1 tsp leavening agent, 1/2 tsp vanilla extract; Compote: 1/2 cup mixed berries (blueberries, raspberries), 1 tbsp lemon juice, 1 tsp chia seeds.

Serves = 2

Mode of Cooking = Skillet; Saucepan

Procedure:

In a bowl, whisk together almond flour, eggs, almond milk, baking powder, and vanilla extract until well combined.

Grease a skillet lightly and heat it to medium. To form each pancake, pour 1/4 cup of the batter. Cook until the top begins to bubble, then turn and finish cooking the other side.

For the compote, simmer the berries with the lemon juice in a saucepan until the berries soften. Add the chia seeds and stir, then cover and let thicken.

Serve pancakes with compote on top.

Nutritional values: 280 calories, 10g protein, 23g fat, 9g net carbs, 6g fiber.

Recipe 2: Spinach and Mushroom Egg White Omelette

P.T. = 15 minutes

Ingr. = 1 cup spinach, 1/2 cup sliced mushrooms, 3 egg whites, 1 tbsp olive oil, salt, and pepper to taste.

Serves = 1

Mode of Cooking = Skillet

Procedure:

Sauté mushrooms in a skillet with olive oil until soft. Add spinach until wilted.

Add the egg whites and salt and pepper to taste. Fold and serve after cooking until set.

Nutritional values: 120 calories, 12g protein, 5g fat, 4g net carbs, 2g fiber.

Recipe 3: Chia Seed Pudding with Cinnamon & Pecans

P.T. = 10 minutes (plus overnight refrigeration)

Ingr. = 3 tbsp. 1 cup of unsweetened almond milk and chia grains, 1/2 tsp cinnamon, 1/4 cup. pecans, crushed, a dash of vanilla extract.

Serves = 2

Mode of Cooking = Refrigeration

Procedure:

Mix chia seeds, almond milk, cinnamon, and vanilla in a bowl.

Refrigerate overnight.

Before serving, top with crushed pecans.

Nutritional values: 190 calories, 6g protein, 14g fat, 8g net carbs, 10g fiber.

Recipe 4: No-Sugar Granola with Greek Yogurt

P.T. = 30 minutes

Ingr. = 1 cup rolled oats and half a cup of chopped nuts (walnuts, almonds), 1/4 cup coconut shreds, 1/4 cup of flax seeds, 1/2 cup Greek yogurt, 1 tablespoon melted coconut oil, small amount of vanilla extract.

Serves = 4

Mode of Cooking = Oven

Procedure:

Preheat oven to 350°F (175°C).

Combine the flax seeds, coconut, nuts, oats, coconut oil, and vanilla.

Place onto a baking sheet, stirring halfway through the 20 minutes of baking.

Serve cooled granola with Greek yogurt.

Nutritional values: 230 calories, 8g protein, 14g fat, 16g net carbs, 4g fiber.

Recipe 5: Vegetable and Cheese Breakfast Muffins

P.T. = 35 minutes

Ingr. = 1 cup mixed vegetables (bell peppers, zucchini), 6 large eggs, 1/2 cup grated cheese (cheddar or feta), salt and pepper to taste, 1 tbsp olive oil.

Serves = 6 muffins

Mode of Cooking = Oven

Procedure:

Preheat oven to 375°F (190°C). Grease muffin tin.

Sauté vegetables in olive oil until soft.

Whisk eggs, salt, and pepper. Add vegetables and cheese.

Pour mixture into muffin tin. Bake for 20-25 minutes or until set.

Nutritional values: 120 calories, 7g protein, 8g fat, 3g net carbs, 1g fiber.

Recipe 6: Steel-cut oats with Fresh Berries

P.T. = 30 minutes

Ingr. = 1 cup steel-cut oats, 2.5 cups water, 1/2 cup mixed fresh berries (blueberries, strawberries), 1 tsp vanilla extract, a pinch of salt.

Serves = 2

Mode of Cooking = Stovetop

Procedure:

In a saucepan, bring the water to a boil. Add salt and steel-cut oats.

Reduce to a simmer for 25 minutes or until the oats are tender, stirring occasionally.

Stir in vanilla extract. Serve with fresh berries on top.

Nutritional values: 170 calories, 6g protein, 3g fat, 28g net carbs, 4g fiber.

Recipe 7: Avocado, Tomato, and Egg Toast

P.T. = 15 minutes

Ingr. = 1 ripe avocado, 2 slices whole grain bread, 1 medium tomato (sliced), 2 large eggs, 1 tbsp olive oil, salt and pepper at will.

Serves = 2

Mode of Cooking = Skillet; Toaster

Procedure:

Toast bread slices until golden brown.

Heat the olive oil in a skillet, so cook the eggs until they are the desired doneness.

Mash avocado and spread on toast. Top with tomato slices and fried egg. Season with salt and pepper.

Nutritional values: 290 calories, 11g protein, 20g fat, 20g net carbs, 9g fiber.

Recipe 8: Strawberry-Kiwi Smoothie (with Stevia)

P.T. = 10 minutes

Ingr. = 1 cup strawberries, 1 kiwi (peeled and sliced), 1 cup unsweet. almond milk, 1 tbsp chia seeds, 1-2 drops liquid stevia (optional for added sweetness).

Serves = 1

Mode of Cooking = Blender

Procedure:

Blend strawberries, kiwi, almond milk, chia seeds, and stevia until smooth.

Serve immediately.

Nutritional values: 140 calories, 4g protein, 4g fat, 24g net carbs, 9g fiber.

Recipe 9: Whole Grain Breakfast Burrito (Turkey & Veggies)

P.T. = 25 minutes

Ingr. = 1 whole grain tortilla, 2 oz lean ground turkey, 1/2 cup mixed veggies (bell peppers, onions), 1 large egg, 1/4 cup shredded cheese, 1 tbsp salsa, 1 tbsp olive oil.

Serves = 1

Mode of Cooking = Skillet

Procedure:

In a skillet, sauté turkey until browned. Add veggies and cook until softened.

Push the turkey-veggie mix to one side and scramble the egg on the other side.

Place tortilla on a plate and layer with turkey-veggie mix, scrambled egg, cheese, and salsa.

Roll into a burrito and serve.

Nutritional values: 310 calories, 20g protein, 12g fat, 30g net carbs, 5g fiber.

Recipe 10: Tofu Scramble with Spinach

P.T. = 20 minutes

Ingr. = 1/2 block firm tofu (crushed), 1 cup spinach, 1/2 tsp turmeric, 1/4 tsp paprika, pepper and salt, 1 tbsp olive oil.

Serves = 1

Mode of Cooking = Skillet

Procedure:

Heat olive oil in a skillet. Add crumbled tofu, turmeric, paprika, salt, and pepper.

Sauté for 7-10 minutes until tofu is golden.

Stir in spinach and cook until wilted.

Serve hot.

Nutritional values: 180 calories, 14g protein, 12g fat, 5g net carbs, 2g fiber.

Recipe 11: Coconut Almond Muffins (Sugar-free)

P.T. = 35 minutes

Ingr. = 1/4 cup unsweet. crushed coconut, 1 1/2 cups almond flour, 2 large eggs, 1/2 cup unsweet. almond milk, 1 tsp leavening agent, 1 tsp vanilla extract, 1-2 drops liquid stevia.

Serves = 6 muffins

Mode of Cooking = Baking

Procedure:

Preheat oven to 350°F (175°C). Line a muffin tin with paper liners.

Combine almond flour, shredded coconut, and baking powder in a bowl.

Whisk together eggs, almond milk, vanilla, and stevia in another bowl.

Combine wet and dry ingredients. Stir until smooth.

A toothpick inserted into the center of the muffin tins should come out clean after 20 to 25 minutes of baking.

Nutritional values: 180 calories, 7g protein, 15g fat, 6g net carbs, 3g fiber.

Recipe 12: Berry and Kale Morning Smoothie

P.T. = 10 minutes

Ingr. = 1 handful kale, half a cup blueberries, half a cup raspberries, 1 cup unsweetened almond milk, 1 tablespoon chia seeds, and one tablespoon honey (optional).

Serves = 1

Mode of Cooking = Blender

Procedure:

Blend blueberries, raspberries, kale, almond milk, chia seeds, and honey (if using) until smooth.

Serve chilled.

Nutritional values: 150 calories, 5g protein, 4g fat, 25g net carbs, 8g fiber.

Recipe 13: Overnight Quinoa & Berry Pots

P.T. = 8 hours 15 minutes (including chilling)

Ingr. = Half a cup of cooked quinoa, 1 cup of unsweet.almond milk, half a cup of mixed fresh berries, 1 tablesp. chia seeds, 1 teaspoon honey, and 1 teaspoon vanilla extract.

Serves = 2

Mode of Cooking = Refrigeration

Procedure:

Combine cooked quinoa, almond milk, chia seeds, honey, and vanilla extract in a bowl.

Split the mixture between two bowls or jars.

Top with fresh berries.

Cover and refrigerate overnight. Stir before serving.

Nutritional values: 180 calories, 6g protein, 4g fat, 30g net carbs, 5g fiber.

Recipe 14: Ham & Veggie Breakfast Casserole

P.T. = 1 hour

Ingr. = 1 cup diced ham, half a cup diced bell peppers, one-fourth cup diced onions, one-fourth cup diced tomatoes, 6 large eggs, one-fourth cup milk, to taste salt and pepper, and half a cup of shredded cheese.

Serves = 4

Mode of Cooking = Baking

Procedure:

Preheat oven to 350°F (175°C).

In a bowl, whisk together the 6 eggs, milk, salt, and pepper.

Add the tomatoes, onions, bell peppers, and ham. Well combine.

Spoon mixture into baking dish that has been greased.

Add cheese shreds on top.

Top with shredded cheese.

Bake for 40-45 minutes or until set and lightly browned.

Nutritional values: 220 calories, 18g protein, 13g fat, 5g net carbs, 1g fiber.

Recipe 15: Mixed Seeds Porridge with a Hint of Vanilla

P.T. = 15 minutes

Ingr. = 1/4 cup flaxseeds, 1/4 cup sunflower seeds, 2 cups unsweet. almond milk, 1 tsp extract from vanilla, 1/4 cup chia seeds, 1-2 drops liquid stevia.

Serves = 2

Mode of Cooking = Stovetop

Procedure:

In a saucepan, mix the chia, flaxseeds, sunflower, and almond milk.

Over low heat, bring to a simmer and stir frequently until thickened.

Take off the heat and add the extract fron vanilla and stevia.

Warm up and serve.

Nutritional values: 280 calories, 9g protein, 20g fat, 15g net carbs, 10g fiber.

Chapter 6: Recipes for Lunch

Recipe 1: Grilled Chicken Salad with Olive Dressing

P.T. = 25 minutes

Ingr. = 1 tablesp. olive oil, 1 cup mixed greens, one-fourth cup pitted olives, one-fourth cup cherry tomatoes, 2 tablesp. feta cheese, Dressing: 1 tablesp. lemon juice, 2 tablesp. chopped olives, 1 tablesp. Dijon mustard, 3 tablesp. olive oil, salt, and pepper.

Serves = 2

Mode of Cooking = Grilling

Procedure:

Preheat grill. Season and drizzle olive oil over the chicken. breasts.Grill until fully cooked.

In a bowl, mix dressing ingredients.

Toss greens, olives, tomatoes, and feta. Slice grilled chicken and place on top. Drizzle dressing and serve.

Nutritional values: 330 calories, 28g protein, 20g fat, 5g net carbs, 2g fiber.

Recipe 2: Lentil & Vegetable Medley

P.T. = 45 minutes

Ingr. = 2 cups aqua, 1 cup dried lentils, 1 chopped onion, 2 minced garlic cloves, one tsp olive oil, salt, and pepper, half a cup diced carrots, half a cup diced celery, and half a cup diced tomatoes.

Serves = 4

Mode of Cooking = Stovetop

Procedure:

In a pot, sauté onions and garlic in oil. Add veggies and lentils.

Add water and season. Simmer until lentils are tender.

Nutritional values: 220 calories, 14g protein, 1g fat, 40g net carbs, 8g fiber.

Recipe 3: Tuna Salad Stuffed Tomatoes

P.T. = 20 minutes

Ingr. = Pair of large tomatoes, 1 can of drained tuna, one-fourth cup each of diced cucumber and celery, 2 tablesp.of Greek yogurt, one-fourth teaspoon of Dijon mustard, salt, and pepper.

Serves = 2

Mode of Cooking = No-cook

Procedure:

Combine tuna, cucumber, celery, yogurt, and mustard in a bowl.

Season. Hollow out tomatoes and stuff with tuna mix.

Nutritional values: 140 calories, 20g protein, 2g fat, 10g net carbs, 2g fiber.

Recipe 4: Whole Grain Veggie Wrap with Hummus

P.T. = 15 minutes

Ingr. = 1 whole grain tortilla, 1 tablesp. hummus, one-fourth cup diced tomatoes, one-fourth cup sliced cucumber, one-fourth cup shredded lettuce, and one-fourth cup sliced bell pepper.

Serves = 1

Mode of Cooking = No-cook

Procedure:

Spread hummus on the tortilla. Top with veggies.

Roll and serve.

Nutritional values: 180 calories, 6g protein, 4g fat, 30g net carbs, 6g fiber.

Recipe 5: Quinoa, Black Bean, and Avocado Bowl

P.T. = 35 minutes

Ingr. =1 sliced avocado, 1cup of black beans, 1 cup of aqua, 1 cup of quinoa, 1 cup of diced tomatoes, 1 cup of corn kernels, Dressing: one tablespoon lime juice, two tablespoons olive oil, salt, and pepper.

Serves = 2

Mode of Cooking = Stovetop

Procedure:

Cook quinoa in water.

In a bowl, mix quinoa, beans, tomatoes, and corn. Top with avocado slices.

Drizzle dressing and serve.

Nutritional values: 310 calories, 10g protein, 16g fat, 35g net carbs, 8g fiber.

Recipe 6: Broccoli & Feta Omelette

P.T. = 15 minutes

Ingr. = 2 cups chopped broccoli florets, 1 tablespoon chopped dill, 1 teaspoon EVOO (extra virgin olive oil), 3 large eggs, and salt and pepper.

Serves = 1

Mode of Cooking = Pan-frying

Procedure:

Heat EVOO in a skillet. Add broccoli and sauté until tender.

Whisk eggs, salt, and pepper. Pour over broccoli.

Sprinkle feta and dill. Cook until set.

Nutritional values: 250 calories, 18g protein, 18g fat, 5g net carbs, 2g fiber.

Recipe 7: Turkey, Cheese & Lettuce Whole Grain Sandwich

P.T. = 10 minutes

Ingr. = 2 slices whole grain bread, 4 slices turkey breast, 1 slice Swiss cheese, 2 lettuce leaves, 1 tbsp mayo (prefer low-fat), 1 tsp Dijon mustard.

Serves = 1

Mode of Cooking = No-cook

Procedure:

Spread mayo and mustard on bread.

Layer turkey, cheese, and lettuce. Top with the second slice.

Nutritional values: 320 calories, 24g protein, 12g fat, 30g net carbs, 6g fiber.

Recipe 8: Spinach & Cherry Tomato Frittata

P.T. = 25 minutes

Ingr. = 4 big eggs, 1 cup spinach, 1/2 cup halved cherry tomatoes, tsp olive oil, salt, pepper, 1/4 cup grated Parmesan cheese

Serves = 2

Mode of Cooking = Baking

Procedure:

Preheat oven to 375°F (190°C). In a skillet, heat EVOO and sauté spinach.

In a bowl, whisk eggs, cheese, salt, and pepper. Add spinach and tomatoes.

Pour the mix into an oven-safe dish. Bake for 20 minutes.

Nutritional values: 220 calories, 16g protein, 15g fat, 4g net carbs, 1g fiber.

Recipe 9: Roasted Veggie Salad with Tahini Dressing

P.T. = 40 minutes

Ingr. = 1/2 cup cut up zucchini, 1/2 cup sliced eggplant, 2 tablespoons EVOO, Dressing: 1 tablespoon lemon juice, 2 tablespoons tahini, minced garlic clove, 1/2 cup sliced bell peppers, salt and pepper.

Serves = 2

Mode of Cooking = Roasting

Procedure:

Preheat oven to 400°F (200°C). Toss veggies in EVOO, salt, and pepper.

Spread on a tray and roast for 25 minutes.

Mix dressing ingredients. Toss with roasted veggies.

Nutritional values: 290 calories, 5g protein, 23g fat, 20g net carbs, 6g fiber.

Recipe 10: Egg Salad with Greek Yogurt & Dill

P.T. = 20 minutes

Ingr. = 1/4 cup Greek yogurt, 2 tablesp. chopped dill, 1 teaspoon Dijon mustard, 4 boiled eggs (chopped), salt, and pepper.

Serves = 2

Mode of Cooking = No-cook

Procedure:

Mix eggs, yogurt, dill, mustard, salt, and pepper in a bowl.

Serve on lettuce leaves or whole grain bread.

Nutritional values: 150 calories, 12g protein, 10g fat, 2g net carbs, 0g fiber.

Recipe 11: Chicken Caesar Salad (Low-Fat Dressing)

P.T. = 25 minutes

Ingr. = 1 grilled and sliced chicken breast, 4 cups chopped romaine lettuce, two tablespoons grated Parmesan cheese, Dressing: 1 minced garlic clove, 1 tsp Worcestershire sauce, 1 tsp Dijon mustard, and 2 tablespoons low-fat Greek yogurt, salt and pepper, 1 tsp lemon juice.

Serves = 2

Mode of Cooking = Grilling

Procedure:

Grill chicken until fully cooked. Allow to rest before slicing.

Mix dressing ingredients in a bowl.

Toss lettuce with dressing. Top with chicken slices and Parmesan.

Nutritional values: 240 calories, 30g protein, 8g fat, 6g net carbs, 3g fiber.

Recipe 12: Sweet Potato & Spinach Curry (Mild)

Ingr. = 1 large sweet potato (cubed), 2 cups fresh spinach, 1 can light coconut milk, 2 tbsp curry powder, 1 onion (sliced), 2 cloves garlic (minced), 1 tbsp EVOO, salt, and pepper.

Serves = 4

Mode of Cooking = Stovetop simmering

Procedure:

In a pot, sauté onion and garlic in EVOO until translucent.

Add sweet potatoes and curry powder. Stir for 2 minutes.

Pour coconut milk and simmer until sweet potatoes are tender.

Add spinach and cook until wilted.

Nutritional values: 210 calories, 4g protein, 12g fat, 22g net carbs, 4g fiber.

Recipe 13: Seared Salmon with Zucchini Noodles

P.T. = 20 minutes

Ingr. = 2 salmon fillets, 2 medium zucchinis (spiralized), 1 tbsp EVOO, 1 clove garlic (minced), lemon zest, salt, and pepper.

Serves = 2

Mode of Cooking = Searing

Procedure:

Heat a pan with 1/2 tbsp EVOO. Sear salmon fillets 3-4 minutes per side.

In another pan, sauté garlic in the remaining EVOO. Add zucchini noodles. Cook for 2-3 minutes.

Serve salmon on top of zucchini noodles with a sprinkle of lemon zest.

Nutritional values: 290 calories, 30g protein, 15g fat, 5g net carbs, 2g fiber.

Recipe 14: Vegan Tempeh & Vegetable Stir Fry

P.T. = 30 minutes

Ingr. = 1 cup cubed tempeh, 2 cups mixed vegetables (bell peppers, broccoli, and snap peas), 2 tablespoons soy sauce, one tablespoon sesame oil, 1 tablesp. maple syrup (or other preferred sweetener), 1 teasp. minced ginger and one minced clove of garlic.

Serves = 2

Mode of Cooking = Stir-frying

Procedure:

In a wok, heat sesame oil. Sauté tempeh until golden.

Add veggies, ginger, and garlic. Stir fry for 5-6 minutes.

Drizzle with soy sauce and maple syrup. Toss until well combined.

Nutritional values: 260 calories, 18g protein, 12g fat, 24g net carbs, 6g fiber.

Recipe 15: Portobello Mushroom Pizza (with Veggie Toppings)

P.T. = 25 minutes

Ingr. = 2 big portobello mushroom caps, One-fourth cup shredded mozzarella (or a vegan substitute) and one-fourth cup marinara sauce, 1/4 cup sliced bell peppers, 1/4 cup sliced olives, 1 tsp EVOO, salt, and pepper.

Serves = 2

Mode of Cooking = Baking

Procedure:

Preheat oven to 375°F (190°C). Remove mushroom stems. Brush caps with EVOO, salt, and pepper.

Spread marinara on each cap. Top with veggies and cheese.

Bake until the cheese is bubbly, about 15 minutes.

Nutritional values: 140 calories, 8g protein, 9g fat, 8g net carbs, 2g fiber.

Recipe 16: Grilled Tofu & Broccoli Salad

P.T. = 30 minutes

Ingr. = 1 cup of pressed and cubed tofu, 2 cups of broccoli florets, 1 tablespoon each of soy sauce, sesame oil, rice vinegar, sriracha, honey (or other preferred sweetener), and sesame seeds (for garnish) are needed.

Serves = 2

Mode of Cooking = Grilling

Procedure:

Marinate tofu cubes in soy sauce, sesame oil, rice vinegar, sriracha, and honey for 15 minutes.

Grill tofu until slightly charred on all sides.

Steam broccoli until tender-crisp.

Mix tofu and broccoli and garnish with sesame seeds.

Nutritional values: 220 calories, 15g protein, 11g fat, 15g net carbs, 4g fiber.

Recipe 17: Stuffed Cabbage Rolls

P.T. = 50 minutes

Ingr. = 8 cabbage leaves, 1 can of diced tomatoes, 1 cup cooked brown rice, half a cup ground turkey, 1 chopped onion, 1 minced garlic clove, 1 tsp olive oil, salt and pepper.

Serves = 4

Mode of Cooking = Baking

Procedure:

Sauté onion and garlic in EVOO until translucent. Add ground turkey and cook until browned.

Mix with brown rice, salt, and pepper.

Place mixture into each cabbage leaf and roll.

Lay rolls in a baking dish and cover with diced tomatoes.

Bake at 375°F (190°C) for 30 minutes.

Nutritional values: 190 calories, 12g protein, 3g fat, 28g net carbs, 5g fiber.

Recipe 18: Spaghetti Squash & Marinara

P.T. = 60 minutes

Ingr. = 1 medium spaghetti squash, 1 cup marinara sauce, 1 tablesp. virgin olive oil extra, 2 cloves of minced garlic, 1 tsp of salt, pepper, and dried basil.

Serves = 4

Mode of Cooking = Baking

Procedure:

Remove the seeds after chopping the spaghetti squash in half. Add EVOO, pepper, and salt, and brush.

Bake at 375°F (190°C) for 40-45 minutes.

Scrape the squash with a fork to get "noodles."

Heat marinara with garlic and basil.

Serve over squash noodles.

Nutritional values: 110 calories, 2g protein, 3.5g fat, 20g net carbs, 4g fiber.

Recipe 19: Lettuce Wrap Tacos

P.T. = 20 minutes

Ingr. = 8 large lettuce leaves, 1 chopped tomato, 1 chopped onion, two minced garlic cloves, 1 tsp cumin, 1 tsp smoked paprika, 1 tbsp extra virgin olive oil, salt, and pepper.

Serves = 4

Mode of Cooking = Sautéing

Procedure:

Sauté onion and garlic in EVOO. Add ground chicken and cook until browned.

Add cumin, smoked paprika, salt, and pepper.

Place mixture into lettuce leaves, then sprinkle diced tomato on top.

Nutritional values: 210 calories, 25g protein, 10g fat, 5g net carbs, 2g fiber.

Recipe 20: Mixed Greens & Tuna Nicoise

P.T. = 15 minutes

Ingr. = 1 can (drained) of tuna, 2 cups mixed greens, 4 small boiled potatoes (quartered), 8 steam-cooked green beans, 1/4 cup olives, and 2 boiled eggs (quartered), How to Dress: 1 clove of minced garlic, 2 tablesp. extra virgin olive oil, one tablespoon red wine vinegar, one teaspoon Dijon mustard, salt, and pepper.

Serves = 2

Mode of Cooking = No cook (Assembly)

Procedure:

Arrange greens on a plate. Top with potatoes, green beans, tuna, olives, and eggs.

Combine the dressing ingredients and drizzle it over the salad.

Nutritional values: 330 calories, 20g protein, 15g fat, 28g net carbs, 4g fiber.

Recipe 21: Quinoa & Roasted Veggie Bowl

P.T. = 45 minutes

Ingr. = 1 cup cooked quinoa, 1 bell pepper, 1 zucchini, 1 chopped red onion, 2 tablespoons extra virgin olive oil, salt, pepper, 1 tsp dried oregano, 2 tablespoons feta cheese, and 1 tablespoon lemon juice.

Serves = 2

Mode of Cooking = Roasting

Procedure:

Toss zucchini, bell pepper, and red onion in EVOO, salt, pepper, and oregano.

Arrange the ingredients evenly on a baking sheet and bake for 25 to 30 minutes at 400°F (205°C).

Serve veggies over quinoa, sprinkle with feta cheese, and drizzle with lemon juice.

Nutritional values: 280 calories, 8g protein, 10g fat, 40g net carbs, 5g fiber.

Recipe 22: Chickpea Salad Sandwich

P.T. = 15 minutes

Ingr. = 1 can chickpeas (drained and mashed), 2 tbsp Greek yogurt, 1 celery stalk (chopped), 1 tbsp dill (chopped), 1 tbsp lemon juice, salt, pepper, 4 slices of WG bread.

Serves = 2

Mode of Cooking = No cook (Assembly)

Procedure:

Mix mashed chickpeas, Greek yogurt, celery, dill, lemon juice, salt, and pepper.

Spread the mixture on 2 slices of bread, and top with the remaining slices.

Nutritional values: 290 calories, 12g protein, 4g fat, 52g net carbs, 10g fiber.

Recipe 23: Stuffed Avocado Bowls

P.T. = 20 minutes

Ingr. = Two mature avocados (peeled and halved), 1 cup grilled chicken (chopped), 1/4 cup cherry tomatoes (halved), 2 tbsp corn kernels, 1 tbsp cilantro (chopped), lime juice, salt, pepper.

Serves = 2

Mode of Cooking = No cook (Assembly)

Procedure:

Mix chicken, cherry tomatoes, corn, cilantro, lime juice, salt, and pepper.

Spoon mixture into avocado halves.

Nutritional values: 330 calories, 20g protein, 23g fat, 18g net carbs, 9g fiber.

Recipe 24: Sweet Potato & Black Bean Tacos

P.T. = 35 minutes

Ingr. = 2 medium sweet potatoes (cubed), 1 can black beans (drained), 1 tsp cumin, 1 tsp smoked paprika, 1 tbsp EVOO, 8 small corn tortillas, 1/2 cup salsa, 1/4 cup Greek yogurt, fresh cilantro for garnish.

Serves = 4

Mode of Cooking = Sautéing

Procedure:

Sauté sweet potato cubes in EVOO until tender; add cumin and smoked paprika. Add the black beans and heat through, stirring.

Serve the mixture in corn tortillas, topped with salsa, a dollop of Greek yogurt, and cilantro.

Nutritional values: 240 calories, 8g protein, 4g fat, 45g net carbs, 7g fiber.

Recipe 25: Vegan Sushi Rolls

P.T. = 40 minutes
Ingr. = 2 cups sushi rice (cooked and cooled), 3 nori sheets, 1 avocado (sliced), 1 cucumber (julienned), 1 bell pepper (julienned), 2 tbsp rice vinegar, soy sauce for dipping.
Serves = 4
Mode of Cooking = No cook (Assembly)
Procedure:

Mix rice with rice vinegar.
On a bamboo sushi mat, spread out a sheet of nori. Onto the nori, apply a thin coating of rice.
On the rice, arrange the slices of bell pepper, avocado, and cucumber.
Using the bamboo mat, roll up the nori and press firmly.
Using a sharp, wet knife, cut the roll into eight pieces.
Serve with soy sauce.
Nutritional values: 210 calories, 5g protein, 4g fat, 40g net carbs, 3g fiber.

Chapter 7: Recipes for Dinner

Recipe 1: Lemon Herb Grilled Chicken with Steamed Veggies

P.T. = 35 minutes

Ingr. = 2 boneless chicken breasts, 1 lemon (zested & juiced), 2 tbsp EVOO, 1 tsp dried oregano, 1 tsp dried basil, 1 cup broccoli florets, 1 cup carrot slices.

Serves = 2

Mode of Cooking = Grilling & Steaming

Procedure:

Marinate chicken in a mixture of lemon zest, juice, EVOO, oregano, and basil for 20 minutes.

Preheat the grill and cook chicken for 6-7 minutes on each side.

Steam broccoli and carrot until tender.

Serve chicken with steamed veggies.

Nutritional values: 280 calories, 28g protein, 13g fat, 9g net carbs, 3g fiber.

Recipe 2: Cauliflower Fried Rice with Shrimp

P.T. = 30 minutes

Ingr. = 1 head cauliflower (riced), 200g shrimp (peeled & deveined), 2 eggs (beaten), 2 chopped green onions and 2 beaten eggs, 1 carrot (diced), 2 tbsp low-sodium soy sauce, 1 tbsp sesame oil.

Serves = 3

Mode of Cooking = Sautéing

Procedure:

Heat sesame oil in a skillet, add shrimp and cook until pink.

Add carrot and sauté for 2-3 minutes.

Push ingredients to the side, pour eggs, and scramble.

Add cauliflower rice, soy sauce, and green onions. Mix and cook until heated through.

Nutritional values: 230 calories, 18g protein, 8g fat, 23g net carbs, 5g fiber.

Recipe 3: Vegan Eggplant Parmesan

P.T. = 50 minutes

Ingr. = 1 big eggplant, sliced; 2 cups tomato sauce; 1 cup vegan mozzarella; one-fourth cup nutritional yeast; one-tsp dried oregano and basil; salt; pepper; and one-tbsp extra virgin olive oil.

Serves = 4

Mode of Cooking = Baking

Procedure:

Preheat oven to 375°F (190°C).

Arrange eggplant slices on a baking sheet, brush with EVOO and season.

Bake for 20 minutes.

Layer sauce, eggplant, cheese, and herbs in a baking dish. Repeat.

Top with nutritional yeast and bake for 25-30 minutes.

Nutritional values: 160 calories, 6g protein, 6g fat, 21g net carbs, 7g fiber.

Recipe 4: Beef & Vegetable Kabobs with Tzatziki Sauce

P.T. = 45 minutes (plus marinating)

Ingr. = 300g beef cubes, 1 bell pepper (cubed), 1 red onion (cubed), 1 zucchini (cubed), marinade: 2 tbsp EVOO, 1 tbsp lemon juice, 1 garlic clove (minced), Tzatziki: 1/2 cup Greek yogurt, 1/4 cucumber (grated), 1 garlic clove (minced), 1 tbsp dill (chopped), salt.

Serves = 3

Mode of Cooking = Grilling

Procedure:

Mix marinade and pour over beef. Marinate for 2 hours.

Skewer beef and veggies alternately.

Grill until beef is cooked.

Mix tzatziki ingredients. Serve kabobs with tzatziki sauce.

Nutritional values: 280 calories, 26g protein, 15g fat, 11g net carbs, 2g fiber.

Recipe 5: Spinach and Ricotta Stuffed Chicken Breast

P.T. = 40 minutes

Ingr. = 2 chicken breasts, 100g ricotta, 1 cup spinach (chopped & steamed), 1 garlic clove (minced), salt, pepper, 1 tbsp EVOO.

Serves = 2

Mode of Cooking = Baking

Procedure:

Preheat oven to 375°F (190°C).

Mix ricotta, spinach, garlic, salt, and pepper.

Make indentations in each chicken breast, then fill them with the ricotta mixture.

Seal with toothpicks, brush with EVOO and season.

Bake for 25-30 minutes.

Nutritional values: 310 calories, 30g protein, 16g fat, 5g net carbs, 1g fiber.

Recipe 6: Stuffed Bell Peppers (Quinoa, Tomatoes, Olives)

P.T. = 1 hour

Ingr. = Add 4 bell peppers (halved and seeds removed), 1/4 cup feta cheese and 1 cup cooked quinoa, 1/2 cup sliced black olives, 1 tablesp. extra virgin olive oil, salt, and pepper.

Serves = 4

Mode of Cooking = Baking

Procedure:

Preheat oven to 375°F (190°C).

Combine quinoa, feta, olives, tomatoes, and extra virgin olive oil.

Stuff the quinoa mixture into each half of a bell pepper.

Put in a baking dish and use foil to cover.

For forty minutes, bake.

Nutritional values: 200 calories, 6g protein, 9g fat, 25g net carbs, 5g fiber.

Recipe 7: Zucchini Lasagna (Meat or Vegetarian)

P.T. = 1 hour 15 minutes

Ingr. = 3 zucchinis (sliced thinly lengthwise), 1 lb ground beef or lentils, 2 cups tomato sauce, 1 cup ricotta, 1 egg, 1/4 cup Parmesan, 1 cup mozzarella, salt, pepper, 1 tsp dried oregano.

Serves = 6

Mode of Cooking = Baking

Procedure:

Preheat oven to 375°F (190°C).

If using beef, brown in a skillet. If using lentils, cook until soft.

Mix ricotta, egg, Parmesan, salt, and oregano.

Layer zucchini, meat/lentils, tomato sauce, and ricotta mixture in a baking dish.

Top with mozzarella. Bake for 45 minutes.

Nutritional values: (With beef) 320 calories, 26g protein, 18g fat, 12g net carbs, 3g fiber.

Recipe 8: Garlic Herb Salmon with Asparagus

P.T. = 30 minutes

Ingr. = 2 salmon fillets, 1 bunch asparagus (trimmed), 2 garlic cloves (minced), 1 tbsp EVOO, 1 lemon (zested & juiced), salt, pepper.

Serves = 2

Mode of Cooking = Grilling

Procedure:

Marinate salmon in garlic, EVOO, lemon zest, and juice for 20 minutes.

Preheat grill. Cook salmon for 5-6 minutes on each side.

Grill asparagus until tender.

Serve salmon with grilled asparagus.

Nutritional values: 280 calories, 30g protein, 13g fat, 8g net carbs, 3g fiber.

Recipe 9: Vegan Thai Tofu Curry

P.T. = 40 minutes

Ingr. = 300g tofu (cubed), 1 can coconut milk, 2 tbsp red curry paste, 1 bell pepper (sliced), 1 carrot (julienned), 1 tbsp EVOO, 1 lime (juiced), salt, fresh basil.

Serves = 4

Mode of Cooking = Sautéing

Procedure:

Heat EVOO in a skillet. Sauté tofu until golden brown.

Add red curry paste and stir.

Add veggies and sauté for 5 minutes.

After adding the lime juice and coconut milk, simmer for 20 minutes.

Garnish with fresh basil.

Nutritional values: 290 calories, 12g protein, 22g fat, 13g net carbs, 3g fiber.

Recipe 10: Slow-cooked lamb with Rosemary & Veggies

P.T. = 6 hours 20 minutes

Ingr. = 500g lamb shoulder, 2 rosemary sprigs, 2 garlic cloves (minced), 1 cup beef broth, 2 carrots (sliced), 1 onion (sliced), salt, pepper, 1 tbsp EVOO.

Serves = 4

Mode of Cooking = Slow-Cooking

Procedure:

Season lamb with salt, pepper, and garlic.

Heat EVOO in a skillet, sear lamb on all sides.

Transfer the lamb to a slow cooker. Add rosemary, carrots, onion, and broth.

Cook on low for 6 hours.

Serve lamb with veggies and sauce.

Nutritional values: 350 calories, 30g protein, 20g fat, 9g net carbs, 2g fiber.

Recipe 11: Vegetable and Bean Chili

P.T. = 50 minutes

Ingr. = 2 cans of rinsed and drained mixed beans, 1 can diced tomatoes, one chopped onion, one diced bell pepper, two minced garlic cloves, one tsp each of cumin, paprika, and chili powder, 1 tablesp. virgin olive oil extra, and salt and pepper are all included.

Serves = 6

Mode of Cooking = Stovetop simmering

Procedure:

Heat EVOO in a pot. Sauté onions, bell pepper, and garlic until translucent.

Add spices and stir.

Mix in beans and diced tomatoes. Simmer for 40 minutes.

Season to taste and serve.

Nutritional values: 220 calories, 10g protein, 2g fat, 40g net carbs, 10g fiber.

Recipe 12: Turkey Meatloaf with a Side of Green Beans

P.T. = 1 hour 10 minutes

Ingr. = 2 cups blanched green beans, half a cup tomato sauce, half a cup finely chopped onion, and half a cup minced garlic cloves, 1 pound ground turkey, 1 egg, and salt and pepper are all included.

Serves = 4

Mode of Cooking = Baking

Procedure:

Preheat oven to 375°F (190°C).

Mix turkey, egg, breadcrumbs, onion, garlic, half the tomato sauce, oregano, salt, and pepper.

Shape into a loaf and place in a baking dish.

Cover the meatloaf with the leftover tomato sauce.

Bake for 50 minutes.

Steam or boil green beans for 10 minutes. Serve alongside meatloaf.

Nutritional values: 320 calories, 28g protein, 10g fat, 25g net carbs, 5g fiber.

Recipe 13: Roasted Vegetable Medley with Quinoa

P.T. = 45 minutes

Ingr. = 1 cup quinoa, 2 cups water, 1 bell pepper (diced), 1 zucchini (chopped), 1 red onion (sliced), 1 carrot (sliced), 2 tbsp EVOO, salt, pepper, 1 tsp dried basil.

Serves = 4

Mode of Cooking = Roasting & boiling

Procedure:

Preheat oven to 400°F (200°C).

Mix veggies with EVOO, salt, pepper, and basil. Spread on a baking sheet.

Roast veggies for 25-30 minutes.

While veggies roast, boil water and cook quinoa as per package instructions.

Mix quinoa with roasted veggies and serve.

Nutritional values: 270 calories, 8g protein, 8g fat, 40g net carbs, 6g fiber.

Recipe 14: Grilled Tofu Steaks with Avocado Salsa

P.T. = 30 minutes

Ingr. = 300g tofu (sliced into steaks), 1 avocado (diced), 1 tomato (diced), 1/4 cup red onion (chopped), 1 lime (juiced), salt, pepper, 1 tbsp EVOO.

Serves = 4

Mode of Cooking = Grilling

Procedure:

Preheat grill.

Brush tofu steaks with EVOO and sprinkle with salt & pepper.

Grill tofu 3-4 minutes on each side.

Mix avocado, tomato, onion, lime juice, salt, and pepper for salsa.

Serve grilled tofu topped with avocado salsa.

Nutritional values: 250 calories, 12g protein, 15g fat, 20g net carbs, 7g fiber.

Recipe 15: Butternut Squash & Chickpea Curry

P.T. = 50 minutes

Ingr. = 1 small butternut squash (peeled and cubed), one can rinsed and drained, 1 onion (sliced), 2 minced garlic cloves, 1 can coconut milk, 2 tablespoons curry powder, salt, pepper, and 1 tablespoon extra virgin olive oil.

Serves = 4

Mode of Cooking = Sautéing & simmering

Procedure:

Heat EVOO in a large skillet. Sauté onion and garlic until translucent.

Add butternut squash and curry powder. Stir and cook for 5 minutes.

Mix in chickpeas and coconut milk. Simmer for 35-40 minutes until squash is tender.

Season with salt and pepper. Serve.

Nutritional values: 340 calories, 9g protein, 20g fat, 35g net carbs, 10g fiber.

Recipe 16: Balsamic Glazed Chicken & Veggies

P.T. = 35 minutes

Ingr. = 4 chicken breasts, 1/4 cup balsamic vinegar, 2 tablespoons honey, and 2 minced garlic cloves, 1 cup of halved cherry tomatoes and one sliced bell pepper, 1 zucchini (sliced), 2 tbsp EVOO, salt, pepper.

Serves = 4

Mode of Cooking = Grilling & sautéing

Procedure:

Mix balsamic vinegar, honey, and garlic for the glaze.

Preheat grill. Brush chicken with half the glaze.

Grill chicken 6-7 minutes each side or until done.

Heat EVOO in a skillet. Sauté veggies until tender.

Before serving, drizzle the remaining glaze over the chicken and vegetables.

Nutritional values: 320 calories, 30g protein, 10g fat, 25g net carbs, 4g fiber.

Recipe 17: Stir-Fried Beef & Broccolini

P.T. = 25 minutes

Ingr. = 300g beef strips, 2 cups broccolini (trimmed), 1 tablespoon each of sesame oil, hoisin sauce, minced garlic cloves, three tablespoons of low-sodium soy sauce, and 2 tablesp. of extra virgin olive oil.

Serves = 4

Mode of Cooking = Stir-frying

Procedure:

Heat EVOO in a wok. Stir-fry beef until browned.

Add garlic and broccolini. Stir-fry for another 5 minutes.

Mix in soy sauce, sesame oil, and hoisin. Cook until heated through.

Serve hot.

Nutritional values: 340 calories, 28g protein, 20g fat, 10g net carbs, 3g fiber.

Recipe 18: Creamy Vegan Tomato Basil Pasta

P.T. = 30 minutes

Ingr. = 300g whole grain spaghetti, 1 can diced tomatoes, 1 cup cashews (soaked for 3 hours), 2 garlic cloves (minced), 1/4 cup fresh basil (chopped), salt, pepper, 1 tbsp EVOO.

Serves = 4

Mode of Cooking = Boiling & blending

Procedure:

Cook pasta as per package instructions.

Blend soaked cashews with 1 cup water to create a creamy consistency.

Heat EVOO in a pan. Sauté garlic for 1 minute.

Add tomatoes, cashew cream, and basil. Simmer for 10 minutes.

Season with salt and pepper. Mix with cooked pasta and serve.

Nutritional values: 480 calories, 15g protein, 20g fat, 60g net carbs, 10g fiber.

Recipe 19: Eggplant & Lentil Curry

P.T. = 50 minutes

Ingr. = 1 large eggplant (cubed), 1 cup dried lentils (rinsed & drained), 1 onion (chopped), 2 garlic cloves (minced), 1 can coconut milk, 2 tbsp curry paste, 1 tbsp EVOO, salt, pepper.

Serves = 4

Mode of Cooking = Sautéing & simmering

Procedure:

Heat EVOO in a pot. Sauté onion and garlic until translucent.

Mix in eggplant and lentils.

Stir in curry paste and coconut milk. Bring to a simmer.

Cook lentils until soft, about 40 minutes.

Add a dash of pepper and salt. Serve.

Nutritional values: 370 calories, 12g protein, 20g fat, 35g net carbs, 15g fiber.

Recipe 20: Vegan Stuffed Bell Peppers

P.T. = 50 minutes

Ingr. = 4 bell peppers (tops removed & seeds discarded), 1 cup quinoa (cooked), Half a cup of corn kernels, one can of rinsed and drained black beans, one tsp paprika,one tsp cumin 1 can tomato sauce, salt, pepper.

Serves = 4

Mode of Cooking = Baking

Procedure:

Preheat oven to 375°F (190°C).

Mix quinoa, beans, corn, cumin, paprika, half the tomato sauce, salt, and pepper.

Fill each bell pepper with the mixture.

Place in a baking dish and pour the remaining tomato sauce around them.

Bake for forty minutes with a foil cover on. For ten more minutes, bake without the cover.

Nutritional values: 290 calories, 10g protein, 3g fat, 55g net carbs, 10g fiber.

Nutritional values: 210 calories, 9g protein, 7g fat, 30g net carbs, 8g fiber.

Recipe 21: Cauliflower & Chickpea Masala

P.T. = 40 minutes

Ingr. = 1 large cauliflower (cut into florets), 1 can chickpeas (drained & rinsed), 1 onion (sliced), 3 garlic cloves (minced), 2 tbsp garam masala, 1 tsp turmeric, 1 can diced tomatoes, 1 cup vegetable broth, 2 tbsp EVOO, salt, pepper.

Serves = 4

Mode of Cooking = Sautéing & simmering

Procedure:

Heat EVOO in a pan. Sauté onion and garlic until translucent.

Add garam masala and turmeric, stirring for 1 minute.

Add cauliflower florets, chickpeas, diced tomatoes, and vegetable broth.

Once the cauliflower is tender, simmer it for 25 to 30 minutes after bringing it to a boil.

Season with salt and pepper. Serve.

Recipe 22: Mushroom & Spinach Polenta

P.T. = 45 minutes

Ingr. = 1 cup polenta, 4 cups vegetable broth, 2 cups spinach (washed & chopped), 2 cups mushrooms (sliced), two garlic cloves (minced), 2 tablesp. nutritional yeast (optional for cheesy flavor), 1 tbsp EVOO, salt, pepper.

Serves = 4

Mode of Cooking = Boiling & sautéing

Procedure:

Fill a pot with vegetable broth and bring to a boil. Gradually whisk in polenta. Reduce heat to low, stirring frequently until polenta is thickened.

Stir in nutritional yeast if using. Season with salt and set aside.

In a skillet, heat EVOO. Sauté garlic and mushrooms until mushrooms are browned.

Add spinach and cook until wilted.

Plate the polenta and top with the mushroom and spinach mixture.

Nutritional values: 230 calories, 6g protein, 5g fat, 40g net carbs, 5g fiber.

Chapter 8: Recipes for Cakes and Desserts

Recipe 1: Almond Flour Chocolate Cake (Stevia Sweetened)

P.T. = 45 minutes

Ingr. = 3 large eggs, ½ cup melted coconut oil, ½ cup unsweetened almond milk, ½ cup unsweetened cocoa powder, ½ tsp baking soda, pinch of salt, two cups almond flour, ½ tsp vanilla extract, and one cup stevia.

Serves = 8

Mode of Cooking = Baking

Procedure:

Preheat oven to 350°F (175°C). Grease an 8-inch round cake pan.

In a bowl, mix almond flour, cocoa powder, baking soda, and salt.

In another bowl, combine eggs, coconut oil, almond milk, vanilla, and stevia.

Mix wet and dry ingredients until smooth.

After filling the pan, bake the batter for 25 to 30 minutes.

Cool before serving.

Nutritional values: 210 calories, 7g protein, 19g fat, 8g net carbs, 5g fiber.

Recipe 2: Berry Gelatin Dessert

P.T. = 2 hours (includes setting time)

Ingr. = 2 cups mixed berries, 2 cups water, 2 tbsp gelatin powder, 2 tbsp stevia.

Serves = 4

Mode of Cooking = Boiling & chilling

Procedure:

In a pot, heat water until hot but not boiling.

Add the powdered gelatin and mix until it dissolves.

Add stevia and mix well.

Place berries in a mold and pour the gelatin mixture over.

Chill in the fridge until set, about 1-2 hours.

Nutritional values: 50 calories, 2g protein, 0g fat, 10g net carbs, 2g fiber.

Nutritional values: 260 calories, 5g protein, 23g fat, 10g net carbs, 4g fiber.

Recipe 3: Coconut Cream Pie (Sugar-free)

P.T. = 1 hour 30 minutes

Ingr. = 1 almond flour crust, 1 can full-fat coconut milk, ½ cup stevia, 1 tsp vanilla extract, ¼ cup unsweetened shredded coconut, 3 egg yolks, ¼ cup arrowroot powder.

Serves = 8

Mode of Cooking = Baking & chilling

Procedure:

Pre-bake almond flour crust in a 9-inch pie pan at 350°F (175°C) for 10 minutes.

In a pot, combine coconut milk, stevia, egg yolks, and arrowroot powder. Heat on medium, until thickened, stir..

Take off the heat and mix in the shredded coconut and vanilla.

Pour filling into the crust and chill until set, about 1 hour.

Recipe 4: Chia & Berry Pudding

P.T. = 10 minutes (plus overnight soaking)

Ingr. = 1-cup almond milk, 1-cup mixed berries, ¼ cup chia seeds, 2 tablespoons stevia, and 1 teaspoon vanilla extract.

Serves = 2

Mode of Cooking = Soaking

Procedure:

In a bowl, combine almond milk and chia seeds.

Add stevia and vanilla extract and stir.

Cover and refrigerate overnight.

Before serving, top with berries.

Nutritional values: 150 calories, 5g protein, 8g fat, 15g net carbs, 10g fiber.

Recipe 5: No-Sugar Apple & Cinnamon Muffins

P.T. = 40 minutes

Ingr. = 2 cups almond flour, 2 apples (diced), 3 eggs, ½ cup unsweetened apple sauce, 1 tsp baking soda, 2 tsp cinnamon, ½ cup stevia, ¼ cup coconut oil.

Serves = 12 muffins

Mode of Cooking = Baking

Procedure:

Preheat oven to 350°F (175°C). Line a muffin tin with paper liners.

Combine cinnamon, baking soda, and almond flour in a bowl.

In another bowl, combine eggs, apple sauce, stevia, and coconut oil.

Mix wet and dry ingredients. Fold in diced apples.

Divide batter among muffin cups.

Remove the toothpick after 20 to 25 minutes of baking.

Nutritional values: 180 calories, 6g protein, 15g fat, 10g net carbs, 4g fiber.

Recipe 6: Lemon Cheesecake with Nut Crust

P.T. = 4 hours (includes chilling time)

Ingr. = For crust: 1 cup mixed nuts (almonds, walnuts, pecans), 3 tbsp coconut oil, 2 tbsp stevia. For filling: 16 oz cream cheese, ½ cup stevia, 2 lemons (zested and juiced), three eggs, and 1 teaspoon vanilla extract.

Serves = 8

Mode of Cooking = Baking

Procedure:

Preheat oven to 325°F (163°C). Grease a 9-inch round springform pan.

Blend nuts, coconut oil, and stevia for the crust. Press onto the bottom of the pan.

Beat cream cheese, stevia, lemon zest, lemon juice, eggs, and vanilla until smooth.

Pour the filling over the crust.

Bake for 40-45 minutes, until set but still slightly jiggly in the center.

When storing in the refrigerator, let it cool fully for at least three hours.

Nutritional values: 380 calories, 8g protein, 34g fat, 8g net carbs, 2g fiber.

Recipe 7: Chocolate Avocado Mousse

P.T. = 10 minutes

Ingr. = ¼ cup unsweetened cocoa powder, ¼ cup stevia, 2 tsp extract from vanilla, and a pinch of salt are combined with 2 ripe avocados.

Serves = 4

Mode of Cooking = Blending

Procedure:

In a blender, combine all ingredients.

Blend until smooth and creamy.

Before serving, let it cool for a minimum of one hour.

Nutritional values: 210 calories, 3g protein, 19g fat, 12g net carbs, 8g fiber.

Recipe 8: Mixed Fruit Tart with Almond Crust

P.T. = 1 hour 30 minutes

Ingr. = For crust: 1 ½ cups almond flour, ½ cup coconut oil, 2 tbsp stevia. For filling: 1 cup mixed berries, 1 cup Greek yogurt, 2 tbsp stevia, 1 tsp vanilla extract.

Serves = 8

Mode of Cooking = Baking & chilling

Procedure:

Preheat oven to 350°F (175°C).

Mix crust ingredients and press into a tart pan. Bake for 10-12 minutes. Cool completely.

Mix yogurt, stevia, and vanilla. Spread over the cooled crust.

Top with mixed berries. Chill for 1 hour before serving.

Nutritional values: 280 calories, 8g protein, 24g fat, 10g net carbs, 4g fiber.

Recipe 9: Pumpkin Spice Cake (Stevia Sweetened)

P.T. = 50 minutes

Ingr. = 1 cup of pumpkin puree, two cups of almond flour, 3 eggs, ½ cup stevia, 1 tsp baking soda, two tsp pumpkin spice, and ½ tsp salt.

Serves = 10

Mode of Cooking = Baking

Procedure:

Preheat oven to 350°F (175°C). Grease a 9-inch round cake pan.

Mix all ingredients until well combined.

Transfer into the ready pan and level the surface.

Remove the toothpick after 35 to 40 minutes of baking.

Cool before serving.

Nutritional values: 200 calories, 8g protein, 17g fat, 8g net carbs, 4g fiber.

Recipe 10: Cacao Nib & Walnut Cookies

P.T. = 30 minutes

Ingr. = 2 cups almond flour, ½ cup cacao nibs, ½ cup chopped walnuts, 3 tbsp coconut oil, ¼ cup stevia, 1 egg, 1 tsp vanilla extract.

Serves = 12 cookies

Mode of Cooking = Baking

Procedure:

Preheat oven to 350°F (175°C). Line a baking sheet with parchment paper.

In a bowl, combine all ingredients until a dough forms.

Scoop out dough, flatten into cookie shapes, and place on the prepared sheet.

Toast the edges for a golden color, about 12 to 15 minutes.

Let cool completely before serving.

Nutritional values: 180 calories, 6g protein, 16g fat, 7g net carbs, 3g fiber.

Recipe 11: Berry Frozen Yogurt Popsicles

P.T. = 4 hours 20 minutes (mostly freezing time)

Ingr. = 2 cups Greek yogurt, 1 cup mixed berries (blueberries, raspberries, strawberries), 3 tbsp stevia, 1 tsp vanilla extract.

Serves = 6 popsicles

Mode of Cooking = Freezing

Procedure:

Blend Greek yogurt, stevia, and vanilla extract until smooth.

Fold in mixed berries.

Pour the mixture into popsicle molds.

Freeze for at least 4 hours until solid.

Nutritional values: 80 calories, 8g protein, 1g fat, 10g net carbs, 1g fiber.

Recipe 12: Flaxseed & Berry Crumble

P.T. = 40 minutes

Ingr. = For filling: 2 cups mixed berries, 2 tbsp stevia. For topping: 1 cup ground flaxseeds, ½ cup almond flour, 3 teaspoon coconut oill, 1 tsp cinnamon, 2 tbsp stevia.

Serves = 6

Mode of Cooking = Baking

Procedure:

Preheat oven to 350°F (175°C).

Mix berries and stevia for the filling and spread in a baking dish.

Crumble all topping ingredients into another bowl.

Sprinkle topping over berry filling.

Bake for bubbly and golden, 25 to 30 minutes.

Nutritional values: 220 calories, 6g protein, 15g fat, 12g net carbs, 8g fiber.

Recipe 13: Vanilla Panna Cotta with Berry Compote

P.T. = 4 hours 20 minutes (includes setting time)

Ingr. = For panna cotta: 2 cups heavy cream, 2 tbsp stevia, 1 tbsp gelatin, 2 tsp vanilla extract. For compote: 1 cup mixed berries, 2 tbsp stevia.

Serves = 4

Mode of Cooking = Chilling & simmering

Procedure:

For the panna cotta, sprinkle gelatin over 2 tbsp cold water and let it bloom for 5 minutes.

Heat cream and stevia on low until warm. Stir in gelatin until dissolved.

Remove from heat and add vanilla.

Pour into molds and refrigerate for at least 4 hours.

For the compote, simmer berries and stevia on low until syrupy.

Once panna cotta is set, top with berry compote.

Nutritional values: 330 calories, 2g protein, 30g fat, 8g net carbs, 1g fiber.

Recipe 14: Cinnamon & Nutmeg Spiced Pears

P.T. = 30 minutes

Ingr. = 4 ripe pears, 2 cups water, ¼ cup stevia, 1 cinnamon stick, ½ tsp nutmeg, zest of 1 lemon.

Serves = 4

Mode of Cooking = Simmering

Procedure:

Peel pears and cut them in half.

In a saucepan, bring water, stevia, cinnamon, nutmeg, and lemon zest to a simmer.

Add pears and poach for 20 minutes or until tender.

Serve warm or chilled with some of the spiced liquid.

Nutritional values: 100 calories, 1g protein, 0g fat, 25g net carbs, 5g fiber.

Recipe 15: Chocolate-Dipped Strawberries (Dark Chocolate)

P.T. = 25 minutes

Ingr. = 1 cup dark chocolate (80% cocoa or higher), 15 fresh strawberries, 1 tbsp coconut oil.

Serves = 15 strawberries

Mode of Cooking = Melting

Procedure:

Combine the coconut oil and dark chocolate and melt them in a double boiler or the microwave.

Coat half or ¾ of each strawberry with melted chocolate by dipping it in it.

Place on parchment paper and allow to set in the refrigerator for 20 minutes.

Nutritional values: 60 calories, 1g protein, 4g fat, 5g net carbs, 2g fiber.

Chapter 9: Recipes for Savory Pies

Recipe 1: Spinach & Feta Pie with Almond Flour Crust

P.T. = 60 minutes

Ingr. = To make the crust, whisk together 1/3 cup melted butter, 1/2 tsp salt, and 2 cups almond flour. For filling: 2 cups spinach, 1 cup crumbled feta, 2 eggs, 1/4 cup chopped dill, add salt, pepper to taste, along with 1/2 cup chopped onions and 2 minced garlic cloves.

Serves = 6

Mode of Cooking = Baking

Procedure:

Preheat oven to 350°F (175°C). Press the dough into a pie dish after combining the ingredients. Cook for ten minutes.

In a skillet, sauté onions and garlic till translucent. Add spinach till wilted.

Mix spinach mixture with feta, dill, and eggs. Season with salt and pepper.

Pour filling into crust. Bake for 40 minutes.

Nutritional values: 340 calories, 15g protein, 28g fat, 10g net carbs, 4g fiber.

Recipe 2: Chicken & Mushroom Pie

P.T. = 90 minutes

Ingr. = One cup heavy cream, two minced garlic cloves, a tablesp. of olive oil, salt, pepper, and pie crust (homemade or purchased from the store) are all needed.

Serves = 6

Mode of Cooking = Baking

Procedure:

Preheat oven to 375°F (190°C).

Sauté onions, garlic, and mushrooms in olive oil. Add chicken and cook till browned.

Add chicken broth and heavy cream. Simmer till sauce thickens. Season.

Pour mixture into pie crust. Cover with another pie crust. Make slits on top.

Bake for 45 minutes.

Nutritional values: 390 calories, 25g protein, 28g fat, 15g net carbs, 1g fiber.

Recipe 3: Vegan Lentil & Vegetable Pie

P.T. = 80 minutes

Ingr. = 2 cups vegetable broth, 1 cup lentils, 1 cup diced carrots, 1 cup peas, one cup diced bell peppers, 1 cup chopped tomatoes, 1 tablespoon olive oil, salt, and pepper, along with a vegan pie crust and all of the above ingredients.

Serves = 6

Mode of Cooking = Baking

Procedure:

Preheat oven to 375°F (190°C).

Sauté veggies in olive oil. Add lentils and broth. Cook till lentils are tender.

Season with salt and pepper.

Pour into pie crust. Cover with another crust. Make slits on top.

Bake for 45 minutes.

Nutritional values: 240 calories, 10g protein, 8g fat, 35g net carbs, 10g fiber.

Recipe 4: Seafood Pie with Cauliflower Topping

P.T. = 70 minutes

Ingr. = 1/4 cup heavy cream, 1 tablesp. butter, salt, pepper, and 1 cup mixed seafood (shrimp, scallops, and fish). Add 2 cups chopped cauliflower florets.

Serves = 6

Mode of Cooking = Baking

Procedure:

Preheat oven to 375°F (190°C).

Sauté onions and garlic in butter. Add seafood. Cook till done.

Boil cauliflower till soft. Mash and mix with heavy cream. Season.

Pour seafood mix in a baking dish. Top with cauliflower mash.

Bake for 35 minutes.

Nutritional values: 220 calories, 20g protein, 12g fat, 10g net carbs, 2g fiber.

Recipe 5: Broccoli & Cheddar Quiche

P.T. = 60 minutes

Ingr. = 1/4 cup of thick cream, 4 eggs, 1 cup cheddar cheese and 2 cups broccoli florets, 1/2 cup of chopped onions, 1 clove garlic, minced, salt and pepper, pie crust.

Serves = 6

Mode of Cooking = Baking

Procedure:

Preheat oven to 350°F (175°C).

Sauté onions, garlic, and broccoli.

In a bowl, whisk eggs, cream, cheese, salt, and pepper.

Add broccoli mix to the pie crust. Pour egg mix over.

Bake for 40 minutes.

Nutritional values: 320 calories, 15g protein, 22g fat, 12g net carbs, 2g fiber.

Recipe 6: Shepherd's Pie with Sweet Potato Topping

P.T. = 90 minutes

Ingr. = 500g ground beef or lamb, 1 cup diced carrots, 1/2 cup peas, 2 minced garlic cloves, 1 chopped onion, and 2 cups beef broth, 2 large sweet potatoes, boiled and mashed, 1 tbsp olive oil, salt and pepper.

Serves = 6

Mode of Cooking = Baking

Procedure:

Preheat oven to 375°F (190°C).

In a pan, sauté onions and garlic in olive oil. Add meat and brown.

Add carrots, peas, and broth. Simmer until thickened. Season.

Pour meat mixture into a baking dish. Top with mashed sweet potatoes.

Bake for 45 minutes.

Nutritional values: 410 calories, 25g protein, 18g fat, 35g net carbs, 5g fiber.

Recipe 7: Tomato, Basil, & Mozzarella Tart

P.T. = 50 minutes

Ingr. = 2 big tomatoes, sliced, 1 cup fresh basil, 1 cup mozzarella, sliced, olive oil, salt and pepper, pie crust.

Serves = 6

Mode of Cooking = Baking

Procedure:

Preheat oven to 375°F (190°C).

Lay tomato slices, mozzarella, and basil on the pie crust.

Drizzle with olive oil and season.

Bake for 35 minutes, or until the cheese is bubbling and the crust is golden.

Nutritional values: 280 calories, 10g protein, 15g fat, 25g net carbs, 2g fiber.

Recipe 8: Zucchini & Goat Cheese Tart

P.T. = 55 minutes

Ingr. = 2 medium zucchinis, sliced thinly, 1 cup goat cheese, 1/2 cup caramelized onions, olive oil, salt and pepper, pie crust.

Serves = 6

Mode of Cooking = Baking

Procedure:

Preheat oven to 375°F (190°C).

Spread caramelized onions on the crust. Layer zucchini slices and dot with goat cheese.

Drizzle with olive oil and season.

Bake for 40 minutes.

Nutritional values: 290 calories, 11g protein, 17g fat, 24g net carbs, 2g fiber.

Recipe 9: Turkey & Veggie Pot Pie

P.T. = 80 minutes

Ingr. = 500g turkey meat, cubed, 1 cup mixed vegetables (carrots, peas, green beans), 2 minced garlic cloves, 1 chopped onion, and 2 cups of chicken broth 1/4 cup cream, 2 tbsp olive oil, pie crust, salt and pepper.

Serves = 6

Mode of Cooking = Baking

Procedure:

Preheat oven to 375°F (190°C).

Sauté onions and garlic in oil. Add turkey, cook till browned.

Add veggies, broth, and simmer. Stir in cream. Season.

Pour into pie crust, cover with another crust.

Bake for 45 minutes.

Nutritional values: 400 calories, 28g protein, 22g fat, 20g net carbs, 3g fiber.

Recipe 10: Vegan Tofu & Spinach Quiche

P.T. = 70 minutes

Ingr. = 1 crumbled block of firm tofu, 2 cups spinach, 1/2 unsweetened almond milk, 1/4 cup black salt (kala namak), one-fourth cup turmeric, pie crust, 1/4 cup nutritional yeast, olive oil, salt, and pepper.

Serves = 6

Mode of Cooking = Baking

Procedure:

Preheat oven to 350°F (175°C).

Sauté spinach in olive oil till wilted.

Blend tofu, nutritional yeast, almond milk, turmeric, and black salt. Mix with spinach.

Pour mixture into pie crust.

Bake for 50 minutes.

Nutritional values: 230 calories, 15g protein, 10g fat, 18g net carbs, 4g fiber.

Recipe 11: Ham, Pineapple, & Cheese Tartlets

P.T. = 45 minutes

Ingr. = 200g diced ham, 1 cup pineapple chunks, 1 cup grated cheddar cheese, mini tartlet shells, 2 tablesp. honey, 1 tablesp. Dijon mustard, salt, and pepper.

Serves = 12 tartlets

Mode of Cooking = Baking

Procedure:

Preheat oven to 375°F (190°C).

Mix ham, pineapple, and cheese in a bowl.

Mix honey and Dijon mustard in a different bowl.

Combine both mixtures and fill each tartlet shell.

Bake for 25 minutes or until golden brown.

Nutritional values: 120 calories, 7g protein, 5g fat, 10g net carbs, 0.5g fiber.

Recipe 12: Mixed Veggie & Cheese Pie

P.T. = 75 minutes

Ingr. = 2 cups mixed vegetables (bell peppers, zucchini, carrots), 1 tablespoon dried oregano, 1 tbsp olive oil, 1/4 cup feta cheese, pie crust, 1 cup grated cheddar cheese salt, and pepper.

Serves = 6

Mode of Cooking = Baking

Procedure:

Preheat oven to 375°F (190°C).

Sauté mixed vegetables in olive oil until slightly softened.

Spread vegetables on the pie crust. Sprinkle with cheese.

Season with oregano, salt, and pepper.

Bake for 40 minutes.

Nutritional values: 300 calories, 10g protein, 18g fat, 24g net carbs, 3g fiber.

Recipe 13: Salmon & Dill Quiche

P.T. = 70 minutes

Ingr. = 300g salmon fillet, 2 tbsp fresh dill, chopped, 4 large eggs, 1/4 cup cream, pie crust, 1 tbsp olive oil, salt and pepper.

Serves = 6

Mode of Cooking = Baking

Procedure:

Preheat oven to 350°F (175°C).

In a pan, cook salmon fillet in olive oil until slightly flaky. Break into pieces.

Whisk together eggs, cream, dill, salt, and pepper.

Spread salmon pieces on pie crust. Pour egg mixture over.

Bake for 50 minutes.

Nutritional values: 320 calories, 21g protein, 20g fat, 14g net carbs, 0.5g fiber.

Recipe 14: Beef & Pea Pie with Whole Wheat Crust

P.T. = 90 minutes

Ingr. = 500g ground beef, 1 cup peas, 1 onion, chopped, whole wheat pie crust, 1 tbsp olive oil, 2 tsp Worcestershire sauce, salt and pepper.

Serves = 6

Mode of Cooking = Baking

Procedure:

Preheat oven to 375°F (190°C).

Sauté onions in olive oil. Add ground beef and brown.

Stir in peas, Worcestershire sauce, salt, and pepper.

Fill pie crust with the mixture.

Top with another pie crust and bake for 45 minutes.

Nutritional values: 420 calories, 30g protein, 22g fat, 25g net carbs, 4g fiber.

Recipe 15: Eggplant & Tomato Layered Pie

P.T. = 80 minutes

Ingr. = 1 tablesp. of olive oil, salt, pepper, Grated Parmesan cheese (1/4 cup), 1/4 cup of basil, and two medium eggplants should all be sliced.

Serves = 6

Mode of Cooking = Baking

Procedure:

Preheat oven to 375°F (190°C).

Arrange alternate layers of eggplant and tomato slices in a baking dish.

Drizzle with olive oil, sprinkle with basil, salt, and pepper.

Top with parmesan cheese.

Bake for 60 minutes or until eggplant is tender.

Nutritional values: 130 calories, 5g protein, 6g fat, 15g net carbs, 5g fiber.

Chapter 10: Recipes for Appetizers

Recipe 1: Cucumber & Hummus Bites

P.T. = 15 minutes

Ingr. = 1 large cucumber, sliced; 200g hummus; paprika; fresh parsley for garnish.

Serves = 6

Mode of Cooking = None (Raw)

Procedure:

Lay cucumber slices flat on a serving plate.

Spoon a dollop of hummus onto each cucumber slice.

Sprinkle with paprika and garnish with parsley.

Nutritional values: 70 calories, 2g protein, 4g fat, 7g net carbs, 2g fiber.

Recipe 2: Stuffed Cherry Tomatoes with Tuna Salad

P.T. = 20 minutes

Ingr. = 20cherry tomatoes, one can of drained tuna, 2 tablesp. of mayonnaise, 1 teaspoon of Dijon mustard, salt, pepper, and fresh dill for garnish.

Serves = 5 (4 tomatoes each)

Mode of Cooking = None (Raw)

Procedure:

Slice the tops off cherry tomatoes and scoop out the insides.

Mix tuna, mayonnaise, and Dijon mustard. Season with salt and pepper.

Fill each tomato with tuna salad.

Garnish with dill.

Nutritional values: 85 calories, 10g protein, 3g fat, 2g net carbs, 0.5g fiber.

Recipe 3: Grilled Zucchini Rolls with Goat Cheese

P.T. = 25 minutes

Ingr. = 2 zucchinis, sliced lengthwise; 200g goat cheese; 1 tbsp olive oil; salt & pepper.Serves = 4

Mode of Cooking = Grilling

Procedure:

Preheat grill to medium-high heat.

After sprinkling salt and pepper on the zucchini slices, drizzle with olive oil.

Cook the slices of zucchini for two to three minutes on each side.

Spread each slice with goat cheese after it has cooled, then roll up.

Nutritional values: 120 calories, 7g protein, 9g fat, 4g net carbs, 1g fiber.

Recipe 4: Shrimp & Avocado Lettuce Wraps

P.T. = 30 minutes

Ingr. = 20 medium shrimps, peeled and deveined; 1 avocado, sliced; 10 lettuce leaves; 1 tbsp olive oil; 1 tsp garlic powder; salt & pepper.

Serves = 5 (2 wraps each)

Mode of Cooking = Pan-frying

Procedure:

Use a skillet over medium-high heat to heat the olive oil.

Season shrimps with garlic powder, salt, and pepper.

Cook shrimps for 2 minutes per side or until pink.

Place shrimp and avocado slices on lettuce leaves and wrap.

Nutritional values: 140 calories, 10g protein, 8g fat, 5g net carbs, 3g fiber.

Recipe 5: Mini Spinach & Cheese Muffins

P.T. = 35 minutes

Ingr. = 1 cup cheddar cheese, 2 cups freshly chopped and grated spinach, 2 large eggs, half a teaspoon baking soda, one cup almond flour, salt, and pepper are all needed.

Serves = 12 mini muffins

Mode of Cooking = Baking

Procedure:

Preheat oven to 375°F (190°C).

In a bowl, mix all ingredients until well combined.

Fill mini muffin tins with the mixture.

Bake for 20 minutes or until golden.

Nutritional values: 85 calories, 4g protein, 6g fat, 2g net carbs, 1g fiber.

Recipe 6: Olive & Feta Stuffed Peppers

P.T. = 20 minutes

Ingr. = 15 mini bell peppers, 100g feta cheese, crumbled; 50g green olives, chopped; 1 tbsp fresh parsley, chopped; 1 tbsp olive oil; salt & pepper.

Serves = 5 (3 peppers each)

Mode of Cooking = Baking

Procedure:

Preheat oven to 375°F (190°C).

Slice the tops off the mini bell peppers and remove seeds.

In a bowl, mix feta, olives, parsley, salt, and pepper.

Stuff each pepper with the feta mixture.

After putting it on a baking sheet and applying an olive oil coat to it, bake it for 10 minutes.

Nutritional values: 110 calories, 4g protein, 9g fat, 4g net carbs, 2g fiber.

Recipe 7: Vegan Spring Rolls with Peanut Sauce

P.T. = 30 minutes

Ingr. = 10 rice paper sheets; 2 cups mixed vegetables (carrot, cucumber, bell pepper), julienned; 200g firm tofu, sliced; 1/4 cup peanut butter; 1 tablespoon lime juice, 1 tablesp. agave nectar, 1 tablespoon sesame oil, and 2 tablespoons low-sodium soy sauce.

Serves = 5 (2 rolls each)

Mode of Cooking = None (Raw)

Procedure:

Prepare the dipping sauce by whisking together peanut butter, soy sauce, lime juice, agave nectar, and sesame oil. Add water to desired consistency. Set aside.

Wet rice paper sheets individually and lay flat.

Place a slice of tofu and a handful of vegetables in the middle.

Roll tightly, folding in the sides.

Serve with peanut sauce.

Nutritional values: 180 calories, 9g protein, 8g fat, 20g net carbs, 2g fiber.

Recipe 8: Chicken Skewers with Yogurt Dip

P.T. = 25 minutes

Ingr. = 300g cubed chicken breast, 1 cup Greek yogurt, 2 tablesp. lemon juice, 1 tablesp. chopped fresh dill, 1 tablesp.olive oil, salt, and pepper.

Serves = 5 (2 skewers each)

Mode of Cooking = Grilling

Procedure:

Preheat grill to medium-high heat.

Skewer the chicken cubes. Add salt and pepper for seasoning, and drizzle with olive oil.

Grill skewers for 5-7 minutes per side or until fully cooked.

For the dip, mix Greek yogurt, lemon juice, dill, salt, and pepper.

Serve skewers with yogurt dip.

Nutritional values: 150 calories, 20g protein, 5g fat, 4g net carbs, 0g fiber.

Recipe 9: Vegetable Platter with Baba Ganoush

P.T. = 40 minutes

Ingr. = 1 large eggplant, 2 tablespoons tahini, minced garlic clove, 2 tablesp. lemon juice, 1 tablesp. olive oil, salt, and pepper. You also need to add assorted raw vegetables (carrots, bell peppers, and cucumbers) for dipping.

Serves = 6

Mode of Cooking = Roasting & Blending

Procedure:

Preheat oven to 400°F (200°C).

Pierce the eggplant several times with a fork. Place on a baking sheet and roast for 30-35 minutes.

Let cool, then peel and place in a blender.

Add salt, pepper, lemon juice, garlic, and tahini. Until smooth, blend.

Present alongside raw vegetables and a drizzle of olive oil.

Nutritional values: 100 calories, 3g protein, 7g fat, 9g net carbs, 4g fiber.

Recipe 10: Smoked Salmon & Cream Cheese Roll-Ups

P.T. = 15 minutes

Ingr. = 200g smoked salmon slices, 100g cream cheese, 1 tablesp lemon zest, 2 tablesp chopped fresh chives, and black pepper.

Serves = 5 (2 roll-ups each)

Mode of Cooking = None (Raw)

Procedure:

Mix cream cheese, chives, lemon zest, and black pepper in a bowl.

Drizzle each slice of smoked salmon with a little of the cream cheese mixture after it has been arranged.

Roll up the salmon slices.

Serve immediately.

Nutritional values: 110 calories, 8g protein, 7g fat, 1g net carbs, 0g fiber.

Recipe 11: Mini Meatballs with Low-Sugar Tomato Dip

P.T. = 40 minutes

Ingr. = 300g lean ground beef, 1 tsp dried oregano, 1 tsp dried basil, 1 egg, 100g of reduced-sugar tomato sauce, 1 minced garlic clove, 1 tablespoon olive oil, salt, and pepper.

Serves = 5 (5 meatballs each)

Mode of Cooking = Pan-frying & Simmering

Procedure:

In a bowl, combine beef, oregano, basil, egg, salt, and pepper. Mix well and form into small meatballs.

In a pan with heated olive oil, cook the meatballs until they are browned all over.

For the dip, heat tomato sauce and minced garlic in a small pot. Simmer for 10 minutes.

Serve meatballs with tomato dip.

Nutritional values: 180 calories, 18g protein, 10g fat, 3g net carbs, 1g fiber.

Recipe 12: Tofu & Vegetable Kabobs

P.T. = 30 minutes (+ marination time)

Ingr. = 200g firm tofu, cubed; 1 bell pepper, cut into squares; 1 zucchini, sliced; 1/4 cup reduced-sodium soy sauce, 1 tablesp. sesame oil, 1 tablespoon agave nectar, and 1 minced garlic clove.

Serves = 5 (2 kabobs each)

Mode of Cooking = Grilling

Procedure:

Combine the soy sauce, sesame oil, agave nectar, and garlic in a bowl.

Marinate tofu cubes in the mixture for at least 1 hour.

Thread tofu and vegetables alternately onto skewers.

Preheat grill to medium heat and grill kabobs for 3-4 minutes on each side.

Serve immediately.

Nutritional values: 140 calories, 8g protein, 7g fat, 12g net carbs, 2g fiber.

Recipe 13: Cheese & Vegetable Stuffed Mushrooms

P.T. = 30 minutes

Ingr. = 15 large mushroom caps, stems removed; 100g grated cheese (e.g., cheddar); 1 small carrot, finely diced; 1 onion (small), finely diced; 1 tbsp olive oil, salt & pepper.

Serves = 5 (3 mushrooms each)

Mode of Cooking = Baking

Procedure:

Preheat oven to 375°F (190°C).

In a pan, heat olive oil and sauté onion and carrot until softened.

Mix in grated cheese and season with salt and pepper.

Spoon the cheese mixture into each cap of mushrooms.

After placing on a baking sheet, bake the mushrooms for 15 to 20 minutes, or until they are soft.

Serve hot.

Nutritional values: 115 calories, 6g protein, 8g fat, 5g net carbs, 1g fiber.

Recipe 14: Vegan Cauliflower & Nut Patties

P.T. = 40 minutes

Ingr. = 1 medium cauliflower, florets separated; 100g mixed nuts (e.g., almonds, walnuts), finely chopped; 2 tbsp chia seeds, soaked in water; 1 tbsp olive oil; 1 tsp cumin; salt & pepper.

Serves = 5 (2 patties each)

Mode of Cooking = Pan-frying

Procedure:

Steam cauliflower florets until tender.

In a bowl, mash cauliflower and combine with nuts, soaked chia seeds, cumin, salt, and pepper.

Form into patties.

In a pan with heated olive oil, cook patties until golden brown on both sides.

Serve warm.

Nutritional values: 170 calories, 5g protein, 14g fat, 9g net carbs, 4g fiber.

Recipe 15: Asparagus Wrapped in Prosciutto

P.T. = 15 minutes

Ingr. = 15 asparagus spears, trimmed; 15 slices of prosciutto; 1 tbsp olive oil; black pepper.

Serves = 5 (3 wrapped spears each)

Mode of Cooking = Pan-frying

Procedure:

Each spear of asparagus has a prosciutto slice wrapped around it.

Prosciutto-wrapped asparagus should be fried in hot olive oil until crisp.

Sprinkle some black pepper on top and serve right away.

Nutritional values: 90 calories, 6g protein, 6g fat, 2g net carbs, 1g fiber.

Chapter 11: Fish and Seafood

Recipe 1: Lemon Butter Grilled Tilapia

P.T. = 20 minutes

Ingr. = 4 tilapia fillets, 2 tablesp. unsalted butter, 1 lemon's zest and juice, 1 minced garlic clove, salt, and pepper.

Serves = 4

Mode of Cooking = Grilling

Procedure:

Preheat grill to medium heat.

In a bowl, mix together butter, lemon zest, lemon juice, and minced garlic.

After adding salt and pepper to the tilapia fillets, brush them with the lemon butter mixture.

Grill fillets for 3-4 minutes on each side until fully cooked.

Serve immediately.

Nutritional values: 200 calories, 23g protein, 11g fat, 1g net carbs, 0g fiber.

Recipe 2: Shrimp Scampi with Zucchini Noodles

P.T. = 30 minutes

Ingr. = 400g peeled and deveined shrimp, 3 zucchinis (spiralized), 2 tsp olive oil, 4 minced garlic cloves, 1/4 tablesp red pepper flakes, salt and pepper, 1/4 cup white wine, 2 tablesp chopped parsley.

Serves = 4

Mode of Cooking = Sautéing

Procedure:

The olive oil should be warmed in a big skillet over medium heat. Add the garlic and red pepper flakes, so cook for one minute.

Cook the shrimp for two minutes on each side, or until they turn pink.

Half-reduce the white wine after adding.

After three minutes, add the spiralized zucchini noodles and continue to sauté.

Add pepper and salt for seasoning, then garnish with chopped parsley.

Serve right away.

Nutritional values: 210 calories, 25g protein, 8g fat, 8g net carbs, 2g fiber.

Recipe 3: Garlic Herb Baked Cod

P.T. = 35 minutes

Ingr. = 4 cod fillets, 3 garlic cloves minced, 2 tablesp olive oil, 1 tsp dried basil, 1 tsp dried oregano, salt & pepper.

Serves = 4

Mode of Cooking = Baking

Procedure:

Preheat oven to 375°F (190°C).

In a bowl, combine minced garlic, olive oil, basil, oregano, salt, and pepper.

Place cod fillets on a baking dish and brush them with the herb mixture.

Bake the fish for 20/25 minutes, or until it is cooked through and flaky.

Serve right away.

Nutritional values: 190 calories, 27g protein, 7g fat, 1g net carbs, 0g fiber.

Recipe 4: Seafood Paella (with Brown Rice)

P.T. = 1 hour

Ingr. = 200g cleaned and deveined shrimp, 200g cleaned and debearded mussels, 100g squid rings, 1 chopped onion, 1 chopped bell pepper, 3 minced garlic cloves, 1/4 teaspoon of saffron threads, 1/2 tsp smoked paprika, 2 tablespoons olive oil, 4 cups fish broth, salt and pepper, 2 tablespoons chopped parsley, and 1 lemon (cut into wedges) are all included in the 300g brown rice dish.

Serves = 6

Mode of Cooking = Simmering

Procedure:

In a big skillet or paella pan, heat olive oil over medium heat. Sauté onion, bell pepper, and garlic until soft.

Add brown rice and stir well, ensuring each grain is coated with oil.

Add saffron, paprika, salt, and pepper. Add the fish broth and heat until it boils.

For 35 to 40 minutes, or until the rice is almost cooked, reduce heat, cover, and simmer.

Put the squid, mussels, and shrimp in. Once the seafood is cooked through and the mussels have opened, continue cooking it covered for a further ten minutes.

Add some chopped parsley as a garnish and serve with lemon wedges.

Nutritional values: 310 calories, 22g protein, 8g fat, 35g net carbs, 3g fiber.

Recipe 5: Tuna & Avocado Salad

P.T. = 15 minutes

Ingr. = 2 cans of tuna (drained), diced avocado, 1/4 cup red onion, 2 tablesp. cilantro, 1 lime, 1 tablesp. olive oil, salt, and pepper.

Serves = 4

Mode of Cooking = Mixing (No heat)

Procedure:

In a bowl, mix together tuna, diced avocado, chopped red onion, and cilantro.

Drizzle with lime juice and olive oil. Mix until well combined.

Season with salt and pepper to taste.

Serve immediately or refrigerate for later use.

Nutritional values: 230 calories, 25g protein, 12g fat, 8g net carbs, 5g fiber.

Recipe 6: Salmon Patties with Dill Sauce

P.T. = 30 minutes

Ingr. = 500g salmon (cooked and flaked), 1/4 cup almond flour, 1 egg, 2 tbsp chopped dill, 1 teasp. lemon juice, Two tablesp olive oil, half a cup Greek yogurt, salt, and pepper.

Serves = 4

Mode of Cooking = Pan-frying

Procedure:

In a bowl, mix salmon, almond flour, egg, 1 tbsp of dill, lemon juice, salt, and pepper.

Form into patties.

Fill a pan with the olive oil and place it over medium heat. Cook patties until golden brown, 3–4 minutes per side.

Whisk the Greek yogurt and the leftover dill together to make the dill sauce in a different bowl.

Serve salmon patties with dill sauce on the side.

Nutritional values: 290 calories, 28g protein, 16g fat, 4g net carbs, 2g fiber.

Arrange asparagus alongside scallops.

Nutritional values: 220 calories, 24g protein, 10g fat, 6g net carbs, 2g fiber.

Recipe 7: Seared Scallops with Asparagus

P.T. = 20 minutes

Ingr. = 12 large scallops, one bunch of trimmed asparagus,2 tablespoons olive oil, two minced garlic cloves, salt, and pepper, along with one lemon (zested and juiced).

Serves = 4

Mode of Cooking = Searing

Procedure:

Heat one tablesp.of olive oil in a pan over medium-high heat. Add a little salt and pepper to the scallops.

They should be put aside after searing the scallops for one to two minutes on each side.

Olive oil and garlic should be added to the same pan. In order to soften the asparagus, sauté it.

Pour in some lemon zest and juice.

Recipe 8: Mussels in White Wine & Garlic Broth

P.T. = 25 minutes

Ingr. = 1kg mussels (cleaned and debearded), 1 cup white wine, 4 garlic cloves (minced), 1 onion (sliced), 2 tbsp butter, 1/4 cup chopped parsley, salt & pepper.

Serves = 4

Mode of Cooking = Simmering

Procedure:

Melt butter in a big pot over a medium heat. Cook the onion and garlic until they become transparent.

Boil the white wine after adding it.

Cover the pot and add the mussels. Sauté the mussels for 5 to 7 minutes, or until they open.

Any mussels that are closed should be thrown out.

Add salt and pepper for seasoning, and sprinkle chopped parsley on top.

Serve immediately with the broth.

Nutritional values: 280 calories, 30g protein, 8g fat, 9g net carbs, 0g fiber.

Recipe 9: Teriyaki Grilled Swordfish

P.T. = 25 minutes (plus marinating time)

Ingr. = 4 swordfish steaks, 1/4 cup soy sauce (low-sodium), 2 tbsp mirin, 1 tbsp honey, 1 garlic clove (minced), 1 tsp grated ginger, sesame seeds (for garnish).

Serves = 4

Mode of Cooking = Grilling

Procedure:

In a bowl, combine soy sauce, mirin, honey, garlic, and ginger to make the teriyaki marinade.

Pour marinade over swordfish steaks and let marinate for at least 30 minutes in the fridge.

Preheat grill to medium-high heat.

Remove swordfish from marinade and grill for 4-5 minutes on each side, or until fully cooked through.

Garnish with sesame seeds.

Serve immediately.

Nutritional values: 260 calories, 30g protein, 6g fat, 9g net carbs, 0g fiber.

Recipe 10: Fish Taco Lettuce Wraps

P.T. = 20 minutes

Ingr. = 500g white fish fillets, 1 tsp cumin, 1 tsp powdered garlic, salt and pepper, 1 tbsp olive oil, 8 large lettuce leaves (like Romaine or iceberg), 1 tsp chili powder, 1 avocado (sliced), 1/4 cup fresh salsa, 1 lime (cut into wedges).

Serves = 4

Mode of Cooking = Pan-frying

Procedure:

Season fish fillets with cumin, chili powder, garlic powder, salt, and pepper.

Melt olive oil in a skillet over a medium-high flame. When the fish is done, add it and cook it for three to four minutes on each side.

Break the cooked fish into smaller pieces with a fork.

Assemble lettuce wraps by placing fish, avocado slices, and salsa onto each lettuce leaf.

Serve with lime wedges on the side.

Nutritional values: 210 calories, 27g protein, 9g fat, 5g net carbs, 3g fiber.

Recipe 11: Seafood Stir Fry with Veggies

P.T. = 30 minutes

Ingr. = 300g mixed seafood (like shrimp, squid, and scallops), 1 bell pepper (sliced), 1 carrot (julienned), 1 zucchini (julienned), 3 tbsp soy sauce (low-sodium), 1 tablesp sesame oil, 2 garlic cloves (minced), 1 tsp grated ginger, 1 tbsp vegetable oil.

Serves = 4

Mode of Cooking = Stir-frying

Procedure:

In a large skillet or wok, heat the vegetable oil to a high temperature. Stir-fry the ginger and garlic for 30 seconds.

Add seafood and stir fry until nearly cooked.

Add vegetables and stir fry for another 3-4 minutes until they're crisp-tender.

Pour in sesame oil and soy sauce, then toss to coat.

Right away, serve.

Nutritional values: 220 calories, 25g protein, 8g fat, 10g net carbs, 2g fiber.

Recipe 12: Prawn & Spinach Curry

P.T. = 35 minutes

Ingr. = 400g prawns (peeled and deveined), 200g spinach (washed and roughly chopped), 1 onion (chopped), 1 tablesp. curry powder, two minced garlic cloves, 1/2 can coconut milk, 1 tbsp olive oil, salt & pepper, fresh cilantro (for garnish).

Serves = 4

Mode of Cooking = Simmering

Procedure:

In a pot, preheat the olive oil over medium heat. Sauté garlic and onions until transparent.

Stir for a minute after adding the curry powder.

After adding the coconut milk, simmer the mixture.

When the prawns turn pink, add them and cook.

Stir in spinach and cook until wilted.

Season with salt and pepper.

Garnish with fresh cilantro before serving.

Nutritional values: 260 calories, 23g protein, 14g fat, 8g net carbs, 3g fiber.

Recipe 13: Grilled Sardines with Lemon & Herbs

P.T. = 20 minutes

Ingr. = 8 fresh sardines (cleaned and gutted), 2 tablesp.olive oil, 1 tablesp. chopped parsley, 1 tablesp. chopped rosemary, salt, and pepper. Zest and juice of 1 lemon.

Serves = 4

Mode of Cooking = Grilling

Procedure:

Preheat grill to medium heat.

Combine the lemon zest, lemon juice, olive oil, parsley, salt, rosemary and pepper in a bowl.

Brush sardines with the herb mixture.

Grill sardines for 2-3 minutes on each side or until cooked through.

Serve immediately.

Nutritional values: 190 calories, 22g protein, 10g fat, 2g net carbs, 0g fiber.

Recipe 14: Clam Chowder (Light Cream Version)

P.T.: 50 minutes

Ingr.:

2 tbsp unsalted butter

1 medium onion (diced)

2 celery stalks (chopped)

2 garlic cloves (minced)

2 large potatoes (peeled and diced)

3 cups vegetable broth

2 pounds fresh clams (cleaned and scrubbed)

1 cup light cream or half & half

Black pepper and salt, freshly ground (to taste)

Fresh chives or parsley (for garnish)

Serves: 4-6

Mode of Cooking: Stovetop

Procedure:

Transform the butter in a large pot over medium heat, so add the onion and garlic and cook until translucent.

Pour in the vegetable broth and potatoes. Once the potatoes are soft, boil them and lower the heat to a simmer.

Stir in clams and cook until they open (discard any that do not open).

Gently stir in the light cream and heat through without letting it boil. Season with salt and pepper.

Serve hot, garnished with chopped chives or parsley.

Nutritional values: 210 calories, 14g protein, 8g fat, 20g net carbs, 2g fiber.

Recipe 15: Baked Fish with Tomato & Capers

P.T. = 30 minutes

Ingr. = 4 fillets of a white fish (like cod or haddock), 2 tomatoes (sliced), 1 tablespoon olive oil, 2 tablespoons capers, one-fourth cup white wine, 2 minced garlic cloves, salt, pepper, and fresh parsley (for garnish).

Serves = 4

Mode of Cooking = Baking

Procedure:

Preheat oven to 375°F (190°C).

Arrange the sliced tomatoes in a baking dish. Add some olive oil drizzle and chopped garlic on top.

Place fish fillets on top of the tomatoes. Pour white wine over the fish, then scatter capers on top.

Season with salt and pepper.

Bake the fish for 20 minutes, covered with aluminum foil in the baking dish, until it is flaky and cooked through.

Garnish with fresh parsley before serving.

Nutritional values: 180 calories, 25g protein, 6g fat, 5g net carbs, 1g fiber.

Chapter 12: Soups and Stews

Recipe 1: Vegetable Lentil Soup

P.T.: 45 minutes

Ingr.:

1 cup green lentils (rinsed and drained)

2 tbsp olive oil

1 onion, chopped

3 carrots, sliced

2 celery stalks, chopped

3 garlic cloves, minced

6 cups vegetable broth

2 tsp cumin

1 bay leaf

Salt & pepper to taste

Fresh parsley for garnish

Serves: 4-6

Mode of Cooking: Stovetop

Procedure:

Bring a large pot of olive oil to a medium temperature. Include onion, carrot, celery, and garlic. Sauté until softened.

Add the bay leaf, cumin, lentils, and vegetable broth. Heat up to a boil.

Once the lentils are tender, cook, covered, for 30 minutes on a simmering heat.

Remove bay leaf. Season with salt and pepper. Garnish with fresh parsley.

Nutritional values: 220 calories, 14g protein, 4g fat, 36g net carbs, 17g fiber.

Recipe 2: Chicken & Veggie Broth

P.T.: 1 hour 30 minutes

Ingr.:

1 lb chicken pieces (bone-in)

2 tbsp olive oil

1 onion, chopped

3 carrots, diced

2 celery stalks, diced

3 garlic cloves, minced

6 cups water

2 bay leaves

Salt & pepper to taste

Fresh parsley, chopped

Serves: 6

Mode of Cooking: Stovetop

Procedure:

In a big pot, warm up the olive oil and gently sauté the garlic, onion, celery, and carrots until they start to soften.

When you add the chicken pieces, they start to brown.

Add water, bay leaves, salt, and pepper.

After coming to a boil, lower heat to a simmer. Cover and cook for 1 hour.

Remove chicken pieces, shred the meat, and return to the pot. Discard bones.

Adjust seasoning and garnish with fresh parsley before serving.

Nutritional values: 180 calories, 24g protein, 7g fat, 5g net carbs, 2g fiber.

Recipe 3: Tomato Basil Soup (Creamless)

P.T.: 40 minutes

Ingr.:

6 ripe tomatoes, diced

2 tbsp olive oil

1 onion, chopped

4 garlic cloves, minced

4 cups vegetable broth

1/4 cup fresh basil, chopped

Salt & pepper to taste

Serves: 4

Mode of Cooking: Stovetop

Procedure:

In a pot, heat olive oil and sauté onion until translucent.

Cook the tomatoes until they start to fall apart after adding the garlic.

After adding the vegetable broth, heat it to a boil and simmer it for 20 minutes.

Smoothly blend soup using an immersion blender.

Stir in fresh basil, season with salt and pepper, and serve.

Nutritional values: 110 calories, 2g protein, 7g fat, 12g net carbs, 3g fiber.

Recipe 4: Beef & Vegetable Stew

P.T.: 2 hours

Ingr.:

1 lb beef chunks

2 tbsp olive oil

1 onion, chopped

3 carrots, sliced

2 potatoes, diced

2 garlic cloves, minced

4 cups beef broth

2 bay leaves

1 tsp thyme

Salt & pepper to taste

Serves: 6

Mode of Cooking: Stovetop

Procedure:

In a pot, brown beef chunks in olive oil. Remove and set aside.

Sauté onion, carrots, and garlic in the same pot until softened.

Return beef to the pot, add potatoes, beef broth, bay leaves, and thyme.

Reduce heat to a simmer after bringing to a boil. Once the beef is tender, cook it covered for one and a half hours.

Season with salt and pepper, and serve.

Nutritional values: 340 calories, 25g protein, 14g fat, 28g net carbs, 5g fiber.

Recipe 5: Vegan Split Pea Soup

P.T.: 1 hour 45 minutes

Ingr.:

1 cup dried green split peas, rinsed

1 tbsp olive oil

1 onion, chopped

3 carrots, sliced

2 celery stalks, diced

4 garlic cloves, minced

6 cups vegetable broth

1 bay leaf

1 tsp cumin

Salt & pepper to taste

Serves: 6

Mode of Cooking: Stovetop

Procedure:

Add the celery, onion, carrots, and garlic to a large pot and sauté over medium heat until soft.

Add split peas, vegetable broth, bay leaf, and cumin.

Once the peas are tender, reduce heat to low, cover, and simmer for one and a half hours.

Discard bay leaf and blend half the soup using an immersion blender. Mix well.

Season with salt and pepper and serve.

Nutritional values: 220 calories, 14g protein, 3g fat, 38g net carbs, 15g fiber.

Recipe 6: Butternut Squash & Ginger Soup

P.T.: 1 hour

Ingr.:

1 medium butternut squash, peeled and cubed

1 tbsp olive oil

1 onion, chopped

2-inch piece ginger, grated

4 cups vegetable broth

1/2 cup coconut milk

Salt & pepper to taste

Serves: 4

Mode of Cooking: Stovetop

Procedure:

Heat olive oil in a pot and sauté onion and ginger until translucent.

Cook the cubed butternut squash for a few minutes after adding it.

After adding the vegetable broth, bring it to a boil.

Simmer until squash is tender, about 30 min.

Blending with an immersion blender, puree the soup until it's extremely smooth.

Add the coconut milk, season with the pepper and salt, and serve.

Nutritional values: 180 calories, 3g protein, 7g fat, 28g net carbs, 6g fiber.

Recipe 7: Clam & Vegetable Soup

P.T.: 50 minutes

Ingr.:

2 cups fresh clams, cleaned

2 tbsp olive oil

1 onion, chopped

3 potatoes, diced

2 garlic cloves, minced

4 cups vegetable broth

1/2 cup white wine

2 tbsp fresh parsley, chopped

Salt & pepper to taste

Serves: 4

Mode of Cooking: Stovetop

Procedure:

Garlic and onion should be sautéed in hot olive oil until they turn transparent.

After adding, cook potatoes for a short while.

Add white wine and veggie broth.

Potatoes should be cooked until they are almost tender by simmering.

When the clams open up, add them and cook.

Before serving, add salt, pepper, and fresh parsley as garnish.

Nutritional values: 210 calories, 15g protein, 7g fat, 24g net carbs, 3g fiber.

Recipe 8: Chicken Noodle Soup (Whole Grain Noodles)

P.T.: 1 hour 15 minutes

Ingr.:

2 chicken breasts, boneless & skinless

2 tbsp olive oil

1 onion, diced

2 carrots, sliced

2 celery stalks, chopped

4 garlic cloves, minced

6 cups chicken broth

2 cups whole grain noodles

2 tsp fresh thyme leaves

Salt & pepper to taste

Serves: 6

Mode of Cooking: Stovetop

Procedure:

In a large pot, the olive oil should be heated over medium heat. Add the garlic, onion, carrots, and celery. Sauté the vegetables until they are soft.

Add the thyme, chicken broth, salt, and pepper along with the chicken breasts.

Once the chicken reaches a boiling point, lower the heat and simmer it for approximately 20 minutes or until it is cooked through.

Take out and shred the chicken, then put it back in the pot.

Cook the whole grain noodles until they are al dente.

If needed, adjust the seasoning before serving.

Nutritional values: 265 calories, 20g protein, 7g fat, 30g net carbs, 4g fiber.

Recipe 9: Spicy Bean & Lentil Soup

P.T.: 1 hour 30 minutes

Ingr.:

1 cup lentils, rinsed

1 cup black beans, soaked overnight and rinsed

1 tbsp olive oil

1 onion, chopped

1 jalapeno pepper, diced

2 tomatoes, diced

6 cups vegetable broth

1 tsp smoked paprika

Salt & pepper to taste

Serves: 6

Mode of Cooking: Stovetop

Procedure:

Heat oil in a large pot and sauté onions until translucent.

Add jalapeno and tomatoes, cooking for an additional 3 minutes.

Add lentils, beans, smoked paprika, and vegetable broth.

After heating to a rolling boil, reduce the heat, cover, and simmer until the beans and lentils are tender, about 1 hour.

Season with salt and pepper, serve warm.

Nutritional values: 240 calories, 15g protein, 3g fat, 38g net carbs, 15g fiber.

Recipe 10: Vegan Pumpkin & Coconut Soup

P.T.: 45 minutes

Ingr.:

4 cups pumpkin puree

1 can (14 oz) coconut milk

1 onion, diced

2 tbsp coconut oil

2 garlic cloves, minced

4 cups vegetable broth

1 tsp curry powder

Salt & pepper to taste

Serves: 4

Mode of Cooking: Stovetop

Procedure:

In a pot, heat coconut oil and sauté onion and garlic until translucent.

Add pumpkin puree, coconut milk, curry powder, and vegetable broth.

Cook for 30 minutes after bringing to a simmer.

Blend until smooth using an immersion blender.

Serve hot after adding salt and pepper for seasoning.

Nutritional values: 265 calories, 5g protein, 18g fat, 27g net carbs, 8g fiber.

Recipe 11: Seafood Gumbo

P.T.: 2 hours

Ingr.:

200g shrimp, peeled & deveined

200g crab meat

200g andouille sausage, sliced

1 onion, chopped

1 bell pepper, chopped

2 celery stalks, chopped

4 garlic cloves, minced

1/4 cup all-purpose flour

4 cups chicken or seafood broth

1 can (14 oz) diced tomatoes

2 tsp Cajun seasoning

2 bay leaves

Salt & pepper to taste

2 tbsp olive oil

Serves: 6

Mode of Cooking: Stovetop

Procedure:

In a large pot, heat olive oil. Add the sausage and cook until browned. Remove and set aside.

In the same pot, add flour to create a roux. Cook until a deep brown color.

Add onions, bell peppers, celery, and garlic. Sauté until softened.

Add broth, diced tomatoes, Cajun seasoning, and bay leaves.

Bring to a simmer, and add shrimp, crab meat, and browned sausage.

Cook for about 1 hour, occasionally stirring. Adjust seasoning and serve hot.

Nutritional values: 365 calories, 28g protein, 16g fat, 25g net carbs, 3g fiber.

Recipe 12: Hearty Turkey & Kale Soup

P.T.: 1 hour 15 minutes

Ingr.:

400g ground turkey

3 cups kale, chopped

1 onion, diced

2 carrots, sliced

3 garlic cloves, minced

5 cups chicken broth

1 tsp dried basil

Salt & pepper to taste

2 tbsp olive oil

Serves: 6

Mode of Cooking: Stovetop

Procedure:

Warm up some olive oil in a pot and add the ground turkey.

Add onions, carrots, and garlic. Sauté until softened.

Pour in the chicken broth, add kale and dried basil.

Simmer until all ingredients are tender, about 1 hour.

Season with salt and pepper, serve warm.

Nutritional values: 250 calories, 20g protein, 12g fat, 15g net carbs, 3g fiber.

Recipe 13: Spinach & Tofu Miso Soup

P.T.: 25 minutes

Ingr.:

300g firm tofu, cubed

2 cups fresh spinach

4 cups water

3 tbsp miso paste

2 green onions, sliced

1 tsp sesame oil

1 sheet nori (seaweed), cut into strips

Serves: 4

Mode of Cooking: Stovetop

Procedure:

In a pot, bring water to a boil.

Lower the heat and add tofu cubes and spinach. Cook for about 5 minutes.

In a separate bowl, mix miso paste with a bit of hot water until smooth.

Add miso mixture to the pot and stir.

Turn off the heat, add sesame oil, green onions, and nori strips.

Serve hot.

Nutritional values: 135 calories, 12g protein, 5g fat, 10g net carbs, 2g fiber.

Recipe 14: Roasted Red Pepper & Tomato Soup

P.T.: 50 minutes

Ingr.:

4 red bell peppers, halved and seeded

4 tomatoes, quartered

1 onion, chopped

3 garlic cloves, minced

4 cups vegetable broth

2 tsp dried basil

Salt & pepper to taste

2 tbsp olive oil

Serves: 4

Mode of Cooking: Oven & Stovetop

Procedure:

Preheat oven to 400°F (200°C).

Place red peppers and tomatoes on a baking sheet. Roast for 30 minutes or until softened.

In a pot, heat olive oil and sauté onions and garlic until translucent.

Add the roasted peppers, tomatoes, vegetable broth, and dried basil.

Bring to a simmer for 10 minutes.

Smoothly puree the soup using an immersion blender. Season with salt and pepper.

Warm up the food.

Nutritional values: 140 calories, 3g protein, 7g fat, 20g net carbs, 4g fiber.

Recipe 15: Vegetable Minestrone with Brown Rice

P.T.: 1 hour 20 minutes

Ingr.:

1 cup brown rice, rinsed

2 carrots, diced

2 celery stalks, chopped

1 zucchini, diced

1 bell pepper, chopped

1 onion, finely chopped

3 garlic cloves, minced

1 can (14 oz) diced tomatoes

1 cup green beans, chopped

5 cups vegetable broth

1 tsp dried basil

1 tsp dried oregano

1/4 cup fresh parsley, chopped

Salt & pepper to taste

2 tbsp olive oil

Serves: 6

Mode of Cooking: Stovetop

Procedure:

In a large pot, heat olive oil. Sauté onions and garlic until translucent.

Add the celery, carrots, bell pepper, and zucchini. Simmer for about 5 minutes, or until veggies begin to soften.

Add the green beans, vegetable broth, and diced tomatoes and stir.

Simmer the mixture after bringing it to a boil. Add the dried oregano, dried basil, and brown rice.

Once the vegetables are soft and the rice is fully cooked, cover and simmer for approximately one hour.

Adjust seasoning with salt and pepper. Stir in fresh parsley before serving.

Serve hot.

Nutritional values: 215 calories, 5g protein, 5g fat, 40g net carbs, 5g fiber.

Conclusion

Reflecting on Diabetic-Friendly Choices

As you've journeyed with us through these diabetic-friendly culinary delights, a pivotal truth emerges: dietary limitations don't equate to a lack of flavor or enjoyment. Harnessing the power of wholesome ingredients and innovative techniques, we've crafted dishes that satisfy the palate and support health. Moreover, the emphasis isn't solely on sugar reduction; it's a holistic approach towards balanced nutrition. Furthermore, exploring this array of recipes provides sustenance and empowerment, fostering a proactive relationship with food beyond mere consumption. As we conclude cherish the resilience inherent in every choice we make for our well-being and savor life's generous offerings, even within constraints.

The Journey Ahead: Sustainable Choices for Life

One lesson stands prominent in our exploration of culinary arts: opting for health-conscious decisions is an ongoing endeavor rather than a mere goal. Our curated recipes stand as a testament to this, showcasing that creativity can indeed thrive within set parameters. This journey isn't about mere elimination but embracing a diet that celebrates both body and soul.

These dietary paths aren't transient trends but integral aspects that shape our daily lives, dictating our overall well-being and emotional states. It's crucial to see beyond mere dietary restrictions and to foster a profound relationship with our food. Each mea becomes a reflection of our dedication and understanding of our body's needs.

Looking ahead, it's pivotal to recognize that every culinary choice is a commitment to a sustainable and health-conscious life. While the path might pose challenges, the rewards are profound. Strive not for perfection but for continuous growth. Listen to your body's cues and react with kindness and understanding. As this chapter concludes, let the knowledge and experiences shared serve as a beacon, illuminating the mindful eating.

Dear readers,

I am grateful that you have joined me on this insightful journey. I hope the recipes and insights shared have sparked a newfound appreciation for the art of mindful eating. Stay curious, stay inspired, and always choose health.

Warmly,
Emma Sage.

Made in the USA
Las Vegas, NV
16 January 2024